SECRET

KANSAS

*A Guide to the Weird,
Wonderful, and Obscure*

Roxie Yonkey

REEDY PRESS

Reedy Press
PO Box 5131
St. Louis, MO 63139
www.reedypress.com

Library of Congress Control Number: 2022949150

ISBN: 9781681064376

Design by Jill Halpin

Unless otherwise indicated, all photos are courtesy of the author or in the public domain.

Printed in the United States of America
23 24 25 26 27   5 4 3 2 1

DEDICATION

In loving memory of my parents, Gene and Mary Lockwood, and my grandparents, Ed and Blanche Batie, and Herbert and Goldie Lockwood.

"Kansas," she says, "is the name of that star."
—Glinda the Good, *The Wonderful Wizard of Oz*

CONTENTS

ACKNOWLEDGMENTS

Anyone writing about Kansas owes the Kansas State Historical Society a debt of gratitude. KanColl: The Kansas Collection is a digitized group of Kansas-themed "nearly lost" books and more. Without KanColl (kancoll.org), I wouldn't have met Miriam Colt Davis of Octagon City. The society's partnership with Newspapers.com and Ancestry.com is also invaluable. Newspapers.com access is limited to the years currently in the public domain. Any Kansan with a driver's license may access these services at kshs.org/ancestry/drivers/dlverify.

So many people across the state have helped shape this book:

I asked Jill Hunter of Visit Ark City for an Etzanoa tour. She and Shannon Martin also introduced me to Dexter and helium. Thank you, Sandy Randel, for an excellent explanation of Etzanoa.

Mary Arlington of the Kansas RV Parks Association and Tiya Tonn of the Kansas Oil Museum suggested I include the Beaumont Hotel and RV Park. Of course, Butler County oil is in the book because Tonn recommended it.

Thank you, Michael Cox and Chad Tuttle of C2T Ranch, for the fascinating Battle of the Saline River tour, and Melissa Dixon and Janet Kuhn of the Hays Convention and Visitors Bureau (CVB) for their support while I explored Ellis County.

Ashland, home of the Big Basin, knows how to make a person feel at home. Thanks to Leann and Losson Pike for the top-notch Clark County tour and to Georgeann and Bill Lang for the writers' paradise called Bear Creek Bed and Breakfast.

Cawker City, next to Glen Elder State Park, is a resort town that doesn't know it. May the citizens' kind and friendly vibe last forever. Thank you, Linda Clover, Lucille Heller, Pam Brummer, Matt Alford, and Julie Agee.

Garden City's Steve Quakenbush and Johnetta Holmes-Hebrlee are the caretakers of all things Finney County history.

Andrew Gustafson of the Johnson County Museum showed me the All-Electric House and the redlining exhibit, which explained a different aspect of the story. He also connected me to Joy Rhodes and Britt Benjamin of the Johnson County Community College Fashion Collection.

I asked for a tour of Alcove Springs near Blue Rapids, and then I learned that the Irving ghost town may have inspired L. Frank Baum's *The Wonderful Wizard of Oz* characters. Thank you, Don Musil, Lynne Turner, and Lori Parker.

No Kansas acknowledgments would be complete without honoring Kansas Tourism and Director Bridgette Jobe. Our state's tourism staff does so much behind the scenes. Public Relations and Communications Manager Colby Sharples-Terry does an excellent job supporting writers. Thank you, all. A special shout-out goes to my friend Mona Carver, Kansas Travel Information Centers Manager.

In 2015, the Travel Industry Association of Kansas honored Visit Salina's Sylvia Rice as the Matriarch of Tourism. She is an inspiration.

Donna Price and Amanda Ravenstein of Geary County CVB let me explore lovely Geary County. Thanks to Fort Riley Museums' director, Dr. Bob Smith, for an enlightening discussion about Camp Funston and the Spanish flu pandemic.

Roger Hrabe of Rooks County Economic Development introduced me to Damar. Brian Newell and Kaylon Roberts gave me detailed tours of their town.

Jessica Sawatski is an amazing ambassador for Wichita, and I would not know nearly as much about the Air Capital of the World without her guidance. I am always eager to visit the state's largest city.

I know the Kansas City stories because of Maila Yang. Kristi Lee tirelessly shines the light on Leavenworth. Thank you.

Thank you, Chris Wilson of Explore Crawford County and Carol Ann Robb of Pittsburg Public Library, for your insight into Crawford County destinations. Thank you, Lelan Dains and Kelly

Mayer, for showing me Emporia, Teacher Town USA, the Gravel Grinding Capital of the World.

I had no idea who Bernard Warkentin was, but I asked Melody Spurney of the Newton CVB to schedule a tour of the Warkentin House Museum. In 10 minutes, I knew Warkentin was a Secret.

Jayne Pearce and the Fort Wallace Memorial Association have turned the Fort Wallace Museum into an outstanding Western museum. I can't wait to see what the museum does next. Thank you for the Sheridan suggestion.

I would not have known Horsethief Reservoir's story without Lea Ann Seiler, then of Hodgeman County Economic Development. Thank you to current reservoir manager Audrey Rupp for the tour and yurt stay.

Ironically, I first learned about Jack Kilby in Texas. I met him again in Great Bend, thanks to Christina Hayes of Explore Great Bend. Plus, she sent me to Underground Ellinwood.

I fell in love with Lindsborg immediately. Thanks, Holly Loftin, for shining a light on Lindsborg. Thank you, Karen Hibbard, for your encouragement, and kudos to you and Marcia Rozell for promoting Manhattan and Purple Pride Worldwide. Thank you to Julie Saddler of Colby CVB and Ann Miner from the Prairie Museum of Art & History. Thanks to First Baptist Church of Goodland for all your support.

My husband, Eric Yonkey, heard each story's first draft.

All the people listed saved me from mistakes. Anything remaining is on me.

Teter Rock

INTRODUCTION

Writer's Digest divides authors into three categories: plotters, pantsers, and plantsers. Plotters write their outlines and follow them. Pantsers (those who write by the seat of their pants) let the story control their book. Plantsers do both.

I am a plantser. Before I started writing, I listed the Secrets I intended to reveal in this book. Captain (Chaplain) Emil Kapaun always was the first Secret. Sergeant Jack Weinstein always was the second. But some of the other Secrets were not on the list.

The Secret discovery process was like untangling a large knot protruding from a wall. For example, I looked into the Bloody Benders' fate after Cherryvale. I pulled a thread, and Frank Bellamy appeared. I didn't know a Kansan had written the Pledge of Allegiance—nor that Francis Bellamy had grabbed the credit.

In my mind, the Johnson County Museum's All-Electric House story was that it was a 1950s show home. However, the story grew more complex after I learned about redlining through the museum's excellent exhibit. The Johnson County Museum connected me with the Johnson County Fashion Collection and the Nerman Museum.

I looked for Mary Elizabeth Lease in St. Paul. She taught in its Catholic school before she became a political firebrand.

On the way to St. Paul, my friend Amy Piper and I passed St. Aloysius Church's ruins in Greenbush. I didn't know that Greenbush or the church existed.

Blue Rapids told me about Dorothy Gale and Irving when I only knew about Alcove Spring. Likewise, the Drug Store Museum led to Mentholatum.

Writing *Secret Kansas: A Guide to the Weird, Wonderful, and Obscure* has been a delightful journey, and I hope you will enjoy following the clues as much as I did while blazing the trail to *Secret Kansas*. Plotters can enjoy the prepared path, while pantsers can savor the vistas around each curve.

A LIFE OF HOPE AND MERCY

How did a priest become a potential saint and a Congressional Medal of Honor winner?

Alone in a filthy death house half a world away from home, Captain (Chaplain) Father Emil Kapaun died a selfless hero. In November 1950, Chinese Communists surrounded Kapaun's unit. Commanders advised the soldiers to escape, if possible, but Kapaun refused. He intended to care for the captives. During the soldiers' march to imprisonment, the chaplain resisted the captors' efforts to break the Americans' morale. When soldiers faltered, he stood between them and their would-be executioners. And then he carried them.

Kapaun snuck out of his barracks at night to scrounge for food in the prison camp. He shared what he found with fellow captives, often refusing to keep anything for himself. He calmly refuted the captors' claims when they tried to coerce the POWs into betraying their faith and country. The camp leaders banned all public prayers, but the chaplain still celebrated Mass. On Easter Sunday, 1951, he held a public service.

Kapaun's tireless efforts broke his body. The POWs tried to preserve and restore their chaplain's health, but without food or medicine, their efforts failed. Finally, the captors

---

CAPTAIN (CHAPLAIN) EMIL J. KAPAUN

WHAT: A heroic candidate for sainthood

WHERE: Visit the museum for the chaplain at 275th St. and Remington Rd.

COST: Donation

PRO TIP: Call 620-381-1689 for a tour appointment

Above: Kapaun carries a soldier. Inset: Kapaun inducted into Pentagon Hall of Heroes. Courtesy of the Department of Defense

came to remove the troublesome priest. As they hauled him to the death house, he blessed them. He died two days later.

Initially, the government awarded the priest a Distinguished Service Cross. However, his men were not satisfied, and in 2013, President Barack Obama presented the Congressional Medal of Honor to the chaplain's nephew, Ray Kapaun. In 2011, the South Korean government honored Kapaun with the Taegeuk Order of Military Merit, its highest military award.

In March 2021, officials in the Army identified the priest's remains, which were sent home to Kansas that September. His remains rest in Wichita's Cathedral of the Immaculate Conception, but his home church, St. John Nepomucene in Pilsen, preserves his Medal of Honor and other artifacts.

In 1993, Pope John Paul II declared Kapaun a Servant of God, the first step to canonization. The church opened the priest's canonization cause in 2008.

A HERO UPGRADED

Can discrimination be remedied?

The United Nations and the Communist nations were negotiating a truce to the Korean War in 1951 when the talks stalled. The United Nations launched a series of combat operations to pressure the opposition. Sergeant Jack Weinstein led First Platoon, Company G, 21st Infantry Regiment, 24th Infantry Division on the afternoon of October 19, 1951. They occupied a position near Hill 533, south of Kumsong, North Korea, during Operation Polar.

Attempting to retake the hill, about 30 Chinese troops counterattacked the 20 Americans, many of whom were already wounded. The Americans had to withdraw, and someone had to cover them. Weinstein volunteered to stay.

Alone, unaided, and under heavy fire, he killed at least six of the enemy with his M-1 rifle. After his ammunition ran out, he threw the enemy's own grenades back at them. His actions stopped their advance and "inflicted numerous casualties."

A few days before, a missile had wounded Weinstein. During this battle that wound reopened and a grenade broke his leg. But he refused to withdraw until another platoon relieved him. That platoon ultimately drove back the enemy.

The US Army reached Line Polar on that same day, and the Communists returned to the cease-fire talks.

SGT. JACK WEINSTEIN

WHAT: Congressional Medal of Honor recipient

WHERE: Cheyenne Valley Cemetery, south of Highway 27-36 intersection, Wheeler

COST: Free

PRO TIP: Visit shortly before sundown to see the sun burnish Weinstein's Medal of Honor frame his son created.

Above: Jack Weinstein (left rear) at Thanksgiving dinner. Inset: Sgt. Jack Weinstein in a tent during the Korean War. Courtesy of the Department of Defense

The Army thought the "Weinstein" name was Jewish. Because of this, the Army awarded him the Distinguished Service Cross (DSC) for his actions on Hill 533. In 2002, Congress required the Army to reopen DSC investigations for soldiers of potential Hispanic or Jewish heritage. The process discovered 24 soldiers who should have received the Medal of Honor, including Weinstein.

Weinstein survived the war but did not live long enough to receive the medal. Instead, his wife, Nancy, received it from President Obama on March 18, 2014, 61 years after the sergeant had earned it.

All service members salute the Medal of Honor recipients. Four sculpted service members permanently render salutes to Weinstein at the Cheyenne Valley Cemetery.

CONLEY SISTERS 1, DEVELOPERS 0

Who saved the Huron Cemetery?

"I will go to Washington and personally defend [the Huron Cemetery]. If I do not, then there is no cemetery in this land safe from sale at the will of the government." —Lyda Conley

Lyda, Helene, and Ida Conley—members of the Wyandot Nation of Kansas—camped at the Huron Cemetery for 40 years to prevent developers from removing their parents' and other ancestors' remains.

Because Lake Huron is far from Kansas City, the "Huron Indian Cemetery" sign seems out of place there. How could a Huron cemetery appear in Kansas City? Because "Huron" was the French name for the Wyandot tribe and Kansas

City is in Wyandotte County.

(The Kansas tribe spells their name "Wyandot," while the Oklahoma tribe spells theirs "Wyandotte.")

In 1843, the Wyandots' Trail of Tears ended in Kansas City. Disease and floods killed numerous tribe members and between 1844 and 1855, the tribe buried 400 people in the cemetery.

Look for the Conley sisters' headstones in the cemetery. Helena's stone reads, "Cursed be the villain that molests their graves."

For more than 125 years, the Wyandots fought developers, but finally, in 1906, an Oklahoma congressman hid permission to sell the cemetery within a 65-page bill. The sale would benefit the Oklahoma Wyandottes, and the congressman would receive a 15 percent commission.

In response, the Conleys moved into "Fort Conley" at their parents' grave. They threatened death to anyone who would disturb them. Lyda attended law school between guard shifts to prepare for a court fight. She graduated in 1902.

Even though developers coveted the site, many local citizens sided with the Conleys. The sisters sued the Secretary of the Interior to protect the cemetery. Eventually, *Conley v. Ballinger* went to the Supreme Court, and Lyda was the first Native American woman to argue a case there.

The court ruled against them, but their fight had attracted an influential champion, US Senator Charles Curtis of Topeka. He belonged to the Kaw tribe. In 1916, Congress funded the Huron Indian Cemetery as a national historic site through Curtis's efforts and, in 2017, the government designated the cemetery a National Historic Landmark. Fittingly, the Conley sisters rest there. They had won.

Left: Huron Indian Cemetery sign.
Below: Eliza, Sarah, Ida Conley gravesites.
Courtesy of Anne Lacy, KCK Public Library

THE HURON CEMETERY'S SAVIORS

WHAT: The first indigenous woman to argue before the US Supreme Court

WHERE: 641 Minnesota Ave., Kansas City

COST: Free

PRO TIP: Visit during daylight hours.

MOTHER
ELIZA BURTON CONLEY
DEPARTED THIS LIFE
JULY 9, 1879

SARAH McINTYRE CONLEY
DEPARTED THIS LIFE
MARCH 7, 1880

IDA CONLEY
DEPARTED THIS LIFE
OCT. 6, 1948

EMANCIPATION BEFORE PROCLAMATION

What was Quindaro?

The Kansas-Nebraska Act started a frantic rush to determine whether Kansas would be a free or slave state. Quindaro provided a free-state port and a means to pry enslaved people from enslavers' control.

The free-staters established towns like Lawrence but needed a Missouri River port.

The Wyandots owned a rocky point beside the river, and the free-staters negotiated for its purchase in 1859. The rocky point was called Quindaro.

Quindaro boomed. The town started the Quindaro–Parkville Ferry and during 1857 and 1858, most of the goods destined for southern Kansas landed there. Meanwhile, the townspeople and local farmers ran an Underground Railroad network. Freedom seekers rode the ferry for secret nighttime river crossings. Occasionally, the conductors confronted slave catchers.

The enslavers sank the ferry in 1861, but in 1862, the Missouri River froze, and enslaved people were able to escape across the ice. They achieved emancipation before the Proclamation.

QUINDARO

WHAT: Freedom seekers' haven in Kansas City

WHERE: Quindaro Ruins Overlook, 27th St. and Sewell Ave., Kansas City

COST: Free

PRO TIP: Together, the Quindaro community and Western University placed John Brown's statue in a memorial plaza. He's carrying a diploma in his right hand, signifying the importance of education.

Eventually, Quindaro declined to the point where the town's investors sued each other for debt repayment. However, Quindaro gained another life when Eben and Jane Blatchly opened a freedman's school. The school developed into Western University in 1881, the first Black college west of the Mississippi. Its music department was a preeminent Black music training center. Its notable graduates included singers and composers Nora Douglas Holt, the first African American woman to receive an American master's degree; Etta Moten Barnett, a US cultural ambassador to Africa; and Eva Jessye, a music director with George Gershwin and a civil rights activist.

The university thrived into the early 20th century, but the prosperity did not last. World War II's draft drained male enrollment and, as a result, the college's final class in 1943 consisted of six females.

In the 1980s, a landfill threatened to engulf Quindaro's remains, but instead, citizens preserved its ruins and built an overlook.

The town received its name from Nancy Brown Guthrie whose Wyandot name Quindaro meant a bundle of sticks. The townspeople interpreted that to mean "strength in unity."

John Brown at Quindaro

JUNE CLEAVER'S PARADISE

What government housing program encouraged segregation?

June Cleaver of *Leave It to Beaver* would feel at home in the All-Electric House. The show portrayed an idyllic American suburban family life. Ward Cleaver carried a briefcase to work while June cared for their home and children, Wally and Theodore "Beaver" Cleaver. The stylish June did housework wearing pearls and heels. The show ran from 1957 to 1963.

In 1953, Kansas City Power & Light installed the All-Electric House in a Prairie Village subdivision. The company installed all the latest electrical conveniences, hoping to increase power sales. More than 62,000 visitors toured the model home, equaling Johnson County's entire population at the time. After two years on display, the house spent 40 years as a home until the family donated it to the Johnson County Museum. The house symbolized the calm life Americans desired after years of economic depression and war.

However, not everyone enjoyed suburbia. The house is the centerpiece of the museum's Becoming Johnson County exhibit, which includes the beautiful neon White Haven Motor Lodge sign owned by a family whose last name was

---

In contrast to Johnson County's blue and green, HOLC maps covered Wyandotte County in red and yellow. Johnson County is still the state's wealthiest, while Wyandotte is the eighth-poorest with an average household income that is half that of some of the neighboring counties.

White. Black travelers felt the sign signified that Johnson County was a whites-only haven. The 1953 *Negro Travelers Green Book* listed no Johnson County options for Black travelers.

The museum's temporary exhibit Redlined explained: In the 1930s, the Home Owners Loan Corporation (HOLC) graded communities' loan worthiness. HOLC maps showed green sectors as "A"-rated. Blue meant "still desirable," yellow indicated "declining," and red sectors were "hazardous."

The rating system was inspired by the Federal Housing Administration (FHA), which administered HOLC. FHA's 1938 *Underwriting Manual* repeatedly warned against the "infiltration . . . of inharmonious racial groups." In other words, it promoted racial segregation. Suburban paradise was only for people who looked like the Cleavers.

Courtesy of Andrew Gustafson, Johnson County Museum

THE ALL-ELECTRIC HOUSE

WHAT: A suburban paradise

WHERE: Johnson County Arts and Heritage Center, 8788 Metcalf Ave., Overland Park

COST: $6 for adults; $5 for seniors aged 60-plus, veterans, and students; and $4 children ages 1–17.

PRO TIP: Kids can travel to the past at the museum's interactive KidScape exhibit.

SEGREGATION DEFEATED

Where was the first successful lunch counter sit-in?

"We are within the law to sit and expect to be served."

—Carol Parks

Carol Parks sat at the lunch counter at Dockum Drug Store in July 1958. She ordered a Coke as if she did that daily. But Parks was Black. At that time, Black customers were required to stand at the counter's end and order food to go. Kansas law mandated equal access, but the law sank under tradition. "We never knew what it was to just sit there and have a glass and dishes," she recalled.

Parks's actions shocked the waitress. Her shock grew when more protestors, including Parks's cousin Ron Walters, filled the counter. Finally, the perplexed manager posted a sign, "This Fountain Temporarily Closed." The activist teens returned—day after day. Dockum belonged to the national Rexall chain. Breaking a chain link might make a national impact. Plus, Wichita "was Mississippi up north," Walters recalled, "so we tried to break it down."

Before the activists took the plunge, they practiced in the basement of St. Peter Claver Catholic Church. Each protester

CHESTER I. LEWIS REFLECTION PARK

WHAT: The first successful sit-in

WHERE: 205 E Douglas Ave., Wichita

COST: Free

PRO TIP: Enjoy a drink at Dockum in the Ambassador Hotel.

The Ambassador Hotel occupies the Dockum site now. The sit-in took place in the current Siena Tuscan Steakhouse.

Lunch counter. Courtesy of Visit Wichita

was to wear her best apparel. No one was allowed to spin in the seats. Chester I. Lewis, the Wichita NAACP President, mentored the sit-in students.

Dockum was losing money as the protest progressed. Some White people boycotted silently. They left when they saw the protestors. Unfortunately, hostile people taunted and threatened the activists. However, three weeks into the sit-in, Dockum's owner told the manager, "Serve them; we're losing money." Lewis called the Dockum chain's vice president to confirm the store's desegregation. The vice president said yes.

Dockum set the sit-in standard. Sit-ins spread from Wichita to Oklahoma City to Greensboro, North Carolina. Eventually, the 1964 Civil Rights Act outlawed segregation. The US Supreme Court upheld the law in *Katzenbach v. McClung* the same year.

SEGREGACIÓN NO MÁS

Who ended Hispanic segregation in Kansas City schools?

In 1925, Kansas City, Kansas, maintained separate high schools for White and Black students. But Hispanic students had no high school. Their school stopped at eighth grade because people believed that they should start work.

Saturnino Alvarado would not accept this, and enrolled his children Jesse and Luz Alvarado at Argentine High. Marcos de Leon and Victorina Perez joined the Alvarados.

"They had tomatoes thrown at my mom and uncle when they approached the front doors of Argentine High School," Rose Marie Mendez, Luz's daughter, said. The children attended school for a week, and then White parents petitioned the board of education to remove them.

The board ignored the petition, and the parents continued to threaten the Hispanic families. The Alvarados, de Leons, and Perezes pulled their children from school to

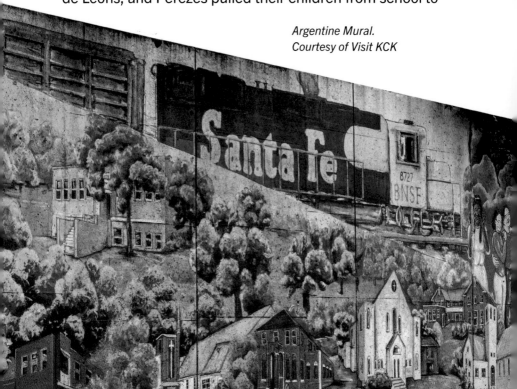

Argentine Mural.
Courtesy of Visit KCK

protect them. When the board offered to send the children to segregated schools, the parents rejected that offer. The board relented but since they offered the students no protection, the parents held their children out of school for a year.

Alvarado owned a shoe-repair shop in the Argentine neighborhood, but he had been born in Michoacan, Mexico. So the parents contacted the Mexican consolate. The consulate pressured the board and Alvarado shared his story with lawyers. "They said, 'We're going to do this *pro bono* so we can find out why they're not letting the Hispanic kids go in through the high school doors,'" Mendez recalled.

Wyandotte County Attorney Harry Hayward added more pressure. He said that the school board's actions "violated the Constitution, international treaty rights . . . and the promise between Mexico and the United States."

In 1926, the de Leon and Alvarado children enrolled in Argentine High. In 1930, they were the school's first Mexican graduates—and earned high marks.

INTEGRATING ARGENTINE HIGH

WHAT: Ending Latinx segregation in education
WHERE: Mid-America Education Hall of Fame, 6565 State Ave.
COST: Free
PRO TIP: View the *Anthology of Argentine* mural at 30th and Woodland, 66103

Argentine High is now Argentine Middle School. AMS named its auditorium for Saturnino Alvarado in 2003, the same year the Mid-America Education Hall of Fame inducted him.

WHITE VS. WHITE SUPREMACY

How did Kansas expel the Ku Klux Klan?

"To make a case against a birthplace, a religion, or a race is wicked, un-American, and cowardly."
—William Allen White

Emporia Gazette Editor William Allen White never intended to run for political office, but then the Ku Klux Klan invaded Kansas, and he had to intervene. Kansas Klan membership had allegedly reached 40,000 in 1922.

White's friend, Governor Henry Allen, had opposed the Klan, but it was the brutalization of Mayor Theodore Schierlmann of Liberty, north of Coffeyville, that caused Allen to investigate the organization. Schierlmann, a Catholic, had refused to rent his combination automobile garage and meeting hall to the Klan. The organization retaliated, kidnapping him from his home. They took him to a spot in the woods where a group of men tied him to a tree and whipped him 30 times in October 1922.

A month later, Black railroaders in Arkansas City refused to join a strike because the unions practiced segregation. The Klan planned an intimidating parade, but Governor Allen objected, saying that would breach the peace. The Klan canceled it.

WILLIAM ALLEN WHITE VS. THE KU KLUX KLAN

WHAT: Expelling the Klan from Kansas

WHERE: William Allen White State Historic Site, 927 Exchange St., Emporia

COST: $6 for adults; $5 for seniors, active military, and college students; $4 for children

PRO TIP: Builders used red Colorado stone to build White's home, naming it Red Rocks.

Red Rocks, William Allen White State Historic Site

Attorney General Richard Hopkins filed two counts against the Klan. One of them alleged that since the Klan did not have a Kansas charter, it could not do business in Kansas. The Kansas Supreme Court agreed, and the Klan appealed to the US Supreme Court.

However, in 1924, neither incumbent Governor Jonathan M. Davis nor challenger Ben Paulen condemned the Klan. So White ran for governor as an independent. "The thought that Kansas [could be] beholden to this hooded gang . . . calls me . . . into this distasteful but necessary task," he wrote. In six weeks, White traveled 2,783 miles and made 104 speeches. He asked voters to elect Charles Griffith as attorney general and Frank Ryan as secretary of state. They would provide two anti-Klan votes on the state's charter board.

White lost to Paulen, but Griffith and Ryan won. The charter board voted 3–0 to deny the Klan's charter. Finally, on February 28, 1927, the US Supreme Court refused to hear the Klan's case. The Klan had to abandon Kansas.

In 1915, Allen commissioned Frank Lloyd Wright to design his Wichita home, the Henry J. Allen House. Allen created the Kansas Court of Industrial Relations in 1920. When White wrote against the court, Allen had him arrested.

ANGEL WITH A BLUE DRESS ON

Who is the Blue Light Lady?

Ephraim and Elizabeth Polly came to Fort Hays around 1867 when Ephraim became an official hospital staff steward. At that time, the steward's wife traditionally became the hospital matron. The couple had arrived at a difficult time; in July 1867, a man from Salina, who was sick with cholera, brought the epidemic from Fort Harker, near Ellsworth, to Fort Hays.

Elizabeth may have had medical training, or maybe she was only a caring person. Whichever the case, she worked tirelessly as the matron of the designated cholera hospital. During the summer, 23 Black Buffalo Soldiers died, but ten more of them recovered. None of the White soldiers died.

Cholera is a bacterial disease spread through dirty water. The bacteria caused severe and deadly dehydration. Because its victims turned blue before they died, it earned the nickname Blue Death.

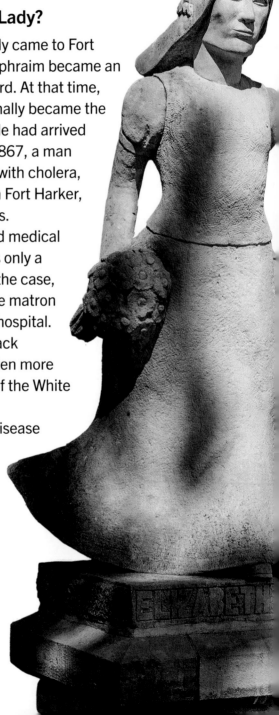

Elizabeth Polly statue.
Courtesy of Brandon Cooley

About 2,000 people inhabited Rome and Hays City, which were close to the fort in those days and the combined death toll caused "a continuous funeral day and night," Simon Motz recalled.

Inevitably, Elizabeth Polly died. She had asked the soldiers to bury her atop Sentinel Hill, because when she was not tending the sick, she walked near the hill to ease her mind. Unfortunately, the top of the hill was too rocky. Instead, the soldiers buried her at its base, wearing a blue dress and a white bonnet. She received full military honors, and the Army marked her grave with four stone posts.

Shortly afterward, four men stole the posts, which was apparently a very bad idea. Each of them soon died violently: one in a gunfight, one hit by a train, and the other two killed in a buggy wreck.

Reports of the Blue Light Lady first appeared in 1917, but it wasn't until the 1950s that a sighting was officially recorded. A policeman reported that he had struck a pedestrian wearing a blue dress with a white bonnet, but when he investigated, no one was there. Since then, many people have reported seeing her floating near the hill, surrounded by blue light.

William F. "Buffalo Bill" Cody founded Rome to compete for a spot on the railroad. Instead, cholera killed its citizens and ruined the town.

HAUNTED SENTINEL HILL

WHAT: The Blue Light Lady

WHERE: From the Hwy. 183 Bypass, go south to Spring Hill Rd. Turn west and drive 1.7 miles. Travel west 1.7 miles. The monument is visible to the north. The burial site is on private property so please do not trespass.

COST: Free

PRO TIP: A marker at Fort Hays State Historic Site tells Polly's story. In 1982, Hays designated Elizabeth Polly Park at 26th and Indian Trail.

CHRISTY'S MYSTERY

Who was Sergeant William Christy?

Mysteries surround the Battle of the Saline River in northern Ellis County. Tsistsis'tas (Cheyenne) and Hinono'eiteen (Arapaho) warriors fought the Buffalo Soldiers there on August 4, 1867. Sergeant William Christy died from a gunshot to the head. He was the Buffalo Soldiers' first casualty. But, then, history lost the battle's location.

In May 2021, Kansas State Historical Society archaeologist Nikki Klarmann certified that the site on C2T Ranch fits the battle's known facts. Ranch historian Michael Cox believes he found Christy's saber handle. This mystery is likely solved.

History records Christy's death, but otherwise, he is a man of mystery.

Christy enlisted in the 10th Cavalry in Harrisburg, Pennsylvania, and arrived at Fort Leavenworth on June 14, 1867. Fort Leavenworth's muster roll did not list any enlisted man's rank, but by August, Christy was a sergeant at Fort Hays. His rank suggests that Christy had had some military experience.

The most likely Christy candidate was from Mercersburg, Pennsylvania, and fought in the famed all-Black 54th Massachusetts Infantry. He saw combat at Fort Wagner and the Battle of Olustee. And then the trail gets weird. In 1864, Christy's brother-in-law, David Demus, wrote his wife about her brother's fate. Demus saw Christy fall, "but I can't tell

BATTLE OF THE SALINE RIVER

WHAT: The Buffalo Soldiers' first casualty

WHERE: C2T Ranch and Campground, 1202 Saline River Rd., Plainville

COST: Varies

PRO TIP: Make an appointment for battlefield tours.

Warriors shot at the cavalry from these bluffs.

where he was shot." They didn't find his body and supposed the Confederates murdered him. Captured Black soldiers didn't become prisoners of war.

If Christy died at the enemy's hands in 1864, who was killed by the enemy in 1867?

Two possibilities: 1) Christy escaped and later reenlisted, or 2) one of the Christy siblings enlisted under his brother's name. A Joseph Christy received wounds at Olustee, but the site of his grave is unknown.

Another candidate, William Christy of Iola, was of military age by 1867. But why would he enlist in Harrisburg instead of at Fort Leavenworth?

Like so much about him, only God knows where Sergeant William Christy's body lies.

BOXCAR FULL OF GRATITUDE

What is the Merci Boxcar?

While Americans had suffered during World War II, the United States did not experience devastation on a par with that suffered in Europe. In 1947, columnist Drew Pearson asked Americans to help Europe recover from the war. He hoped for an 80-car Friendship Train.

The *Wichita Daily Eagle* organized the southwestern states' contribution, which included nearly 200 boxcars. Kansas donated more than 40 cars, including five carloads of wheat from a Ford County farmer. The train left Los Angeles on November 7, 1947, and picked up the Kansas contributions along the way.

In New York, the 700-car train received a ticker-tape parade before it embarked on the SS *American Leader*, renamed the *Friend Ship*. Americans had donated $40 million worth of food, clothes, and medicine. The train arrived in France on December 18, 1947.

In 1949, the French people sent 49 boxcars full of gifts to the United States and christened them the Merci Train (*Merci* means "thank you" in French). Each state received one, and Washington, DC, and the Territory of Hawaii shared the other.

French President Vincent Auriol gave a Sèvres vase to Kansas Governor Frank Carlson. Carlson later donated it to the Kansas State Historical Society in Topeka. The society owns several other Merci gifts. See more of the gifts at the Wamego Public Library and the Prairie Museum of Art & History, Colby.

Kansas "Merci" boxcar

Wichita became the Merci Train's Kansas distribution point. The city displayed the boxcar for 10 days, attracting more than 40,000 visitors. Then the boxcar toured 120 Kansas towns before it reached Hays on Armistice Day 1949. Hays celebrated with a parade and acceptance ceremony.

The train contained pottery, porcelain, crystal, woodwork, church bells, bonnets, costumes, historical documents, musical records, books, and children's letters. Sometimes the giver added a note. The boxcar remained at Fort Hays State University. Eventually, American Legion Post 173 moved the deteriorating boxcar to their grounds to preserve it. In 1993, Hays built Veterans Park, where the car sits under a protective canopy.

MERCI BOXCAR

WHAT: The French sent gifts to America

WHERE: Hays Veterans Memorial Park, 1305 Canterbury, Hays

COST: Donation

PRO TIP: The interior holds military memorabilia. Call the numbers on the boxcar for a tour.

HOME OF VETERANS DAY

How can we honor all veterans?

The guns of World War I fell silent at 11 a.m. on November 11, 1918, the 11th hour of the 11th day of the 11th month. Eventually, the day received the title Armistice Day. The Great War was supposed to be the War to End All Wars. If it had lived up to that notion, November 11 would still be named Armistice Day.

The optimism about war's elimination was misplaced, and the world went to war again in 1939. John Cooper of Emporia died in action in 1944. Shrapnel killed him instantly, and the army buried him in the American cemetery in Limey, France. His grieving uncle, Alvin J. King, worked to honor all those who had served in America's wars, not only those who served in World War I.

King lobbied Emporia's veterans' organizations—the American Legion, Veterans of Foreign Wars, AmVets, and War Dads—to change Armistice Day to Veterans Day. He also enlisted support from Emporia's congressman, Ed Rees. His passion project became a reality on November 11, 1953. At 11 a.m., sirens, church bells, and power-plant whistles sounded the beginning of All Veterans Day in Emporia. When the signal fell silent, two drum-and-bugle corps played "Taps."

Then the festivities began. Governor Edward F. Arn proclaimed, "This is a wonderful thing. It should be done in every city of the nation." Arn's recommendation came true. Rees proposed a bill changing Armistice Day to Veterans

ALL VETERANS MEMORIAL

WHAT: Honoring all veterans

WHERE: 931 S Commercial St., Emporia

COST: Free

PRO TIP: Visit during daylight hours.

Home of Veterans Day sign

Day. Dwight Eisenhower, the Kansan in the White House, signed HR7786 into law on June 1, 1954. Rees and King watched the ceremony.

In 2003, Representative Jerry Moran, R-Kansas, sponsored a House Concurrent Resolution to recognize King as the founder of Veterans Day and Emporia as the holiday's founding city. Visitors come to Emporia from all over the US every November 11 to continue the tradition.

Emporia's All Veterans Memorial Park holds a memorial for Congressional Medal of Honor recipient Grant Timmerman. His remains rest in the National Memorial Cemetery of the Pacific in Honolulu.

ARCHITECT OF THE GI BILL

What was the GI Bill?

Harry Colmery joined the Army Air Service in 1917 and instructed World War I pilots at Texas air bases. Though far from the front, Colmery sympathized with the veterans. He began working to improve their care as soon as he left the service. After he received his honorable discharge in 1919, he became active in the newly founded American Legion. He soon moved and set up a law practice with the father of a friend in Topeka, Kansas.

Colmery watched thousands of desperate veterans and their families march to Washington, DC, in 1932. The "Bonus Army" hoped the government would pay their service bonuses early to help them survive the Great Depression's worst year. Colmery was appalled when the Army drove them out and burned their huts and belongings.

When America entered World War II, an editorial in the *North Topekan* newpaper vowed that the nation would help veterans return to civilian life, and Colmery's 1944 GI Bill would help veterans make that transition. It also powered America's postwar economic expansion. Colmery joined a committee to help Congress pass veterans legislation in 1944. He drafted the GI Bill in longhand on Mayflower Hotel stationery.

His bill included six benefits. Three became the best known: funds for education and training, loan guarantees, and unemployment pay for up to a year. President Franklin Roosevelt signed it into law on June 22, 1944.

Within seven years, eight million veterans used the GI Bill. American degree holders doubled between 1940 and 1950. By July 1956, nearly half of World War II's 16 million veterans had received training through the GI Bill.

Harry Colmery statue

The Servicemen's
Readjustment Act of 1944

HARRY W. COLMERY

WHAT: Author of many veterans benefits

WHERE: Harry W. Colmery Memorial Plaza, 919 S Kansas Ave., Topeka

COST: Free

PRO TIP: Seven statues in downtown Topeka recognize contributors to the city's history and development. Among others, Colmery joins philanthropist Ichabod Washburn, railroad magnate Cyrus K. Holliday, and editor Arthur Capper.

The home loans helped veterans when they started families. They purchased 20 percent of all postwar homes, providing unparalleled prosperity for decades. Congress expanded the bill several times to help veterans from all subsequent American wars.

Topeka dedicated the Harry W. Colmery Memorial Plaza on the GI Bill's 75th anniversary. The Colmery Plaza salutes six World War II—era veterans who represent each military branch. The same veterans wear their postwar professional clothes in relief behind his statue.

In 2019, President Donald Trump posthumously awarded Colmery the Presidential Medal of Freedom. The Topeka veterans hospital, the Colmery-O'Neil VA Medical Center, bears his name.

HEAR US ROAR

How did a women's march improve American mine safety?

Long before Helen Reddy sang, "I am woman, hear me roar," Southeast Kansas women's actions roared throughout the nation. They marched to demand better pay and safer conditions for their miner husbands and sons. The marchers went against the era's prevailing norms for female behavior. At that time, women were supposed to refrain from political action. The *New York Times* mockingly dubbed these women the Amazon Army, but they wore the title as a badge of honor.

The trouble began after World War I when coal prices collapsed and mining companies cut the miners' pay. Governor Henry Allen had created the Court of Industrial Relations to arbitrate labor disputes, but union leader Alexander Howat ignored it. He defied President Woodrow Wilson, Allen, and United Mine Workers President John L. Lewis to lead his miners to strike. Because of Howat's actions, Allen jailed him, and Lewis deposed him as the local leader.

In response, the miners' wives, mothers, sisters, daughters, and sweethearts joined a mass meeting in Franklin's Miners Hall on December 11, 1921. The following day, in the bitter cold, thousands of women and children marched from coal camp to coal camp. The marchers waved American flags and sang patriotic songs to prove they were loyal citizens who only wanted fair treatment.

THE AMAZON ARMY

WHAT: Marching for miners' rights

WHERE: 701 S Broadway St., Franklin

COST: Donation

PRO TIP: Walk the world-record sidewalk that runs between Franklin and Arma. It's reputed to be the world's longest sidewalk connecting two towns.

Solidarity *mural*

Despite the flags, Allen deployed the Kansas National Guard. The Crawford County Sheriff arrested 49 of the women. When their cases came to court, they pled guilty and paid fines ranging from $1 to $200, plus court costs. Howat called off the strike on January 12, 1922.

Mary Skubitz helped lead the Amazon Army. Before she left to march each day, she instructed her 14-year-old son Joe on how to prepare the day's bread. Joe later became a congressman. Congressman Skubitz served for 16 years and helped to pass three crucial mining safety acts.

When Pittsburg needed a public library, the city approached steel magnate and strikebreaker Andrew Carnegie for grant funds. The area's miners would only accept the funds if Carnegie's name were not in the library's title. The mural *Solidarity* on the library's second floor honors the Amazon Army.

INFIDELITY

Why is a vault standing in a pasture?

Cattle graze around an abandoned grocery-store vault—the last remnants of Stone City, a mining camp. Of course, the vault was not always so lonely, but, like many mining camps, Stone City faded away when the minerals were gone.

Before it faded, Stone City wrote its name in the catalog of mining disasters. At 12:06 p.m. on December 13, 1916, an explosion ripped through the Fidelity No. 9 mine, and 20 miners died. Fifteen of them lived in Stone City. The investigation showed that miner Mike Urisk had inadvertently tapped a methane pocket in a coal seam. The methane ignited and exploded the black powder, killing Urisk and 19 others.

After the explosion, 35 miners escaped. Rescue crews found another 10 men who were sick from toxic gases. Gas also overcame one rescuer, who had to leave the mine. Fidelity No. 9 stood only half a mile from Stone City, and the

STONE CITY

WHAT: An abandoned mining camp

WHERE: NW Weir Rd. and NW 40th St., Scammon

COST: Free, but stay outside the fence.

PRO TIP: Look for miners' names at the Miners Memorial at Immigrant Park in Pittsburg.

news spread quickly. Two miners' sons, Lyrton Hey and Ludy Windsor, were among the first bodies to come up the elevator shaft. They might have escaped, but instead, the men had returned to find their fathers, William Hey and William "Hutt" Windsor. The Windsors lost yet another family member, 17-year-old Frank Windsor. A third father-and-son pair, Matt and Charles Roth, also died in the explosion.

The rescue and recovery required 12 hours. Every time another load cleared the shaft, the families surged forward to identify the recovered loved one. When John Fry's body came up, his bride of three weeks attempted to jump into the mine. Others restrained her. As her husband and two sons' bodies cleared the mine, the *Pittsburg Kansan* reported, "It will be a sad Christmas indeed at the home of Mrs. W. H. [Anna] Windsor."

Incredibly, the mine reopened only two weeks later.

Does the vault still weep?

Alexander Howat of the miners union and W. A. Brandenburg of Pittsburg State University headed relief efforts for the miners' families.

Stone City remains in a pasture

WELCOME TO THE JUNGLE

How did a Kansas publisher spawn the FDA and encourage reading?

Kansas has a conservative reputation, but sometimes its citizens defy expectations. At one time, Girard published the socialist newspaper An *Appeal to Reason.* Their presses later produced the "Little Blue Books."

J. A. Wayland brought the newspaper to Girard in 1897. By 1913, its circulation had topped 750,000. Special editions sold millions of copies. Its clout attracted luminaries like Jack London, Helen Keller, Mary Harris "Mother" Jones, and Presidential candidate Eugene Debs.

Coeditor Fred Warren commissioned Upton Sinclair's classic novel *The Jungle.*

First, the newspaper serialized the story, but the response was poor. The *Appeal* canceled the series, but the revised

THE LITTLE BLUE BOOKS

WHAT: A socialist newspaper and press

WHERE: Girard History Museum, 300 S Summit St., Girard

COST: Donation

PRO TIP: In 1868, Dr. Charles Strong shot a deer and established Girard where it fell. A deer sculpture on the Crawford County Courthouse marks the site.

The *Appeal's* large circulation gave Girard a Carnegie library and a first-class post office. Haldeman-Julius Printing continued to publish books until a 1978 fire.

book became a hit in 1906. Sinclair's story about Chicago meatpacking plants disgusted the nation, including President Theodore Roosevelt. As a result, Roosevelt pushed Congress to pass the Food and Drug Act, the foundation for the Food and Drug Administration. Sinclair had hoped to highlight the workers' plight, but instead, he had improved food safety. "I aimed at the public's heart and hit it in its stomach," he said.

The book enriched Sinclair, but the *Appeal*'s staff suffered. Woodrow Wilson's administration repressed socialism, and circulation plummeted. Then Wayland's wife died. The *Appeal* could no longer navigate the commercial jungle—or so Wayland believed. He committed suicide and Warren resigned soon afterward.

Then Emanuel Haldeman-Julius and his wife, Marcet, bought the paper. The new owners pivoted to book publishing—with a twist. Their 3.5-inch by 5-inch Little Blue Books, produced on cheap paper, initially cost 25 cents but eventually sold for a nickel. The publications sold 350–500 million copies.

The books covered mainstream topics like how-to manuals, history, and advice. But they also discussed controversial issues. When the owners questioned FBI Director J. Edgar Hoover, he retaliated by investigating them. Eventually, a federal court convicted Haldeman-Julius of tax evasion. A month later, on July 31, 1951, Emanuel died in his swimming pool.

Little Blue Book printing blocks

THE ULTIMATE TAX PROTEST

Why is a team of horses pulling a bank across the plains?

Many Kansas counties warred over county seat status, but only one, Grant County, moved its seat to avoid taxes.

Ulysses's promoters had approved $36,000 in bonds to ensure it became the county seat. That's over $85 million in 2022 dollars. The leftover funds built a courthouse and a flimsy school. In 1888, Ulysses won the county seat prize over Appomattox. The promoters had founded Ulysses in boom times, but booms often turn to busts. So it was in Grant County. By 1900, two-thirds of the population had fled. The last bank closed in October 1894, and no one opened another for over a decade. No one collected taxes; therefore, no one was paying the bonds.

Old Ulysses townsite marker

Then in 1908, when Ulysses had only 100 residents, the bonds came due. The city's debt had more than doubled, and the court ruled that the citizens must pay. Consequently, city property taxes skyrocketed 600 percent, and personal property taxes jumped 362 percent. After a year of these terrible taxes, the citizens started the ultimate tax protest. They bought a quarter of land three miles away, out of the school district, and surveyed it for a new townsite. Then, in February 1909, they started moving their city's architecture.

Citizens loaded their buildings onto wagons and skids, carving the bulkiest structures, including the Hotel Edwards, into sections. Each hotel section required 60 horses. Imagine the parade of buildings moving down the trail. Three months later, the citizens had left the bondholders with only the land they had purchased. Since the bonds had paid for the courthouse and school, those buildings remained in Old Ulysses. Imagine the bondholders' distress when they discovered that the rest of the town had absconded!

In November, the new city became the county seat. Only a sculptured silhouette of horses pulling a bank across the plains marks Old Ulysses.

OLD AND NEW ULYSSES

The Edwards Hotel's center is part of the Historic Adobe Museum, 300 E Oklahoma Ave., Ulysses 67880.

WHAT: Moving a town to escape taxes

WHERE: Three miles east of Ulysses on Hwy. 160

COST: Free

PRO TIP: Wagon Bed Spring is half an hour southwest of Ulysses. It was the first reliable water source along the Santa Fe Trail's *Jornada del Muerto* (Journey of the Dead Man).

Ulysses Town Site 1885-1909

THE TAXLESS TOWN

How did Colby avoid taxing its citizens for nearly two decades?

On October 22, 1909, an engineer told the Colby Commercial Club that installing city water and power would cost $45,000. The city council scheduled a bond election for early January. The *Colby Tribune* supported the project. The paper devoted its entire front page and part of the back page to the election. The editor predicted that Colby would vote against the bonds. "We think it will be a big mistake," he said.

The newspaper interviewed anonymous citizens. One doubted Colby "had anyone competent to cope . . . with water works." A week later, the paper was more optimistic. "We . . . feel that the better judgment of our citizens will prevail." Male citizens approved the bond 189–44. (Women could not vote in bond elections for another two years.)

The utility staff rapidly disproved their critics. Colby's power requirements expanded quickly, and the city had to upgrade. The city installed two more engines in 1921. The new engines enabled Colby to supply the Thomas County communities of Brewster, Levant, Gem, Rexford, and Selden.

The power plant recouped all its investments, and sales continued to grow. City coffers grew, too. To manage the surplus, the city cut rates. In 1928, Colby's city council

COLBY CITY HALL

WHAT: How power paid a town's taxes

WHERE: Prairie Museum of Art & History, 1905 S Franklin Ave., Colby

COST: $8 for adults, $6 for seniors, and $2 for children aged 6–16

PRO TIP: Stretch your legs on the Colby Walking Trail. Its trailhead is a block north of the Prairie Museum. It runs beside the Colby Event Center and around Colby Community College.

Colby City Hall

waived city taxes for all its citizens. As a result, citizens' overall tax burden dropped 40 percent, even with state and national taxes. The waiver lasted until the 1940s.

Unfortunately, all good things must end. Central Kansas Power (CKP) of Hays built a better Colby power plant in 1945. Consequently, the other Thomas County communities switched to CKP.

Even so, the City of Colby tried to extend the tax-free times. When their power plant needed new engines, the city issued bonds rather than taxing the citizens. However, the competition finally required the city to assess taxes.

The city managed to stay tax-free throughout the Great Depression. When the municipality needed a new city hall, it received funds through the Works Progress Administration, and the WPA workers quarried its exterior limestone south of Monument in Logan County.

LESS CORN AND MORE HELL

Who inspired Kansas farmers to "raise less corn and more hell?"

Mary Elizabeth Lease did not advise farmers to "raise less corn and more hell," in so many words, but she thought it was a "right good bit of advice." She was nearly six feet tall, taller than most men, and enjoyed a deep, rich voice. The height enabled her to project her voice to large halls. The *Wellington Daily Journal* said she had a "bass voice with whiskers on it." William Allen White of the *Emporia Gazette* said she could "recite a multiplication table and set people to hooting."

Mary Elizabeth Clyens taught at St. Paul's Osage Mission for three years until she married Charles Lease in 1873. Three times, the Leases lost their farm. They produced a good

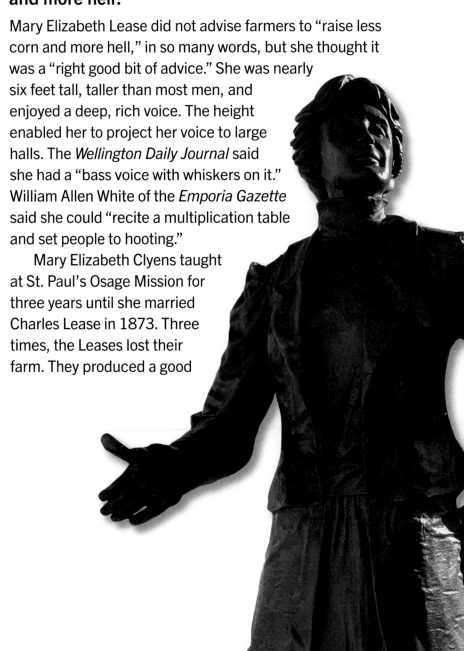

corn crop in their third attempt, but the railroads, banks, and others took all the profits. The Leases failed again.

She stopped raising corn and started raising hell.

The family moved to Wichita in 1884, where Mary Elizabeth became a laundress. She studied law by reading notes on the wall while she scrubbed. She passed the bar exam and became a professional speaker the following year. When advocacy groups formed a new political party, she named them the People's Party or the Populists. That summer, she raged against those who trampled the little man. While she was touring, Senator John J. Ingalls said, "Women don't belong in politics."

MARY ELIZABETH LEASE

WHAT: A female political firebrand

WHERE: Across the street from the Bob Brown Expo Hall on S Cancun St., Wichita

COST: Free

PRO TIP: Visit during daylight hours. Her speaker's pillar recounts her life's story.

Mary Elizabeth Lease proved Ingalls wrong. She helped the Populists elect the attorney general, five of seven congressmen, and enough legislators to replace Ingalls in the US Senate. (Direct election of senators would not come until 1913.) Then, in 1892, Populists considered sending Lease to the US Senate, 20 years before Kansas women could vote. Instead, Joseph Pulitzer's *New York World* hired her in 1897, and she moved to New York. She also represented the city's poor for free.

Lease and eight other women formed the Hypatia Club in January 1886. The club erected Lease's statue in 2001. Hypatia was one of the state's oldest women's clubs until it disbanded in 2012.

TO SPITE YOUR FACE

How did Finney County acquire a nose?

"Do we live in Garfield County or . . . nowhere?"
—*Garfield County Call*, July 8, 1887

Becoming a county seat meant survival, so towns fought to secure the coveted status. People died in physical fights over it in Gray, Stevens, and Wichita counties. However, despite all these controversies, only Garfield County disappeared from the map.

Two towns, Eminence and Ravanna, fought for the Garfield County seat. However, the state's constitution specified that a valid county had to cover 432 square miles. Had the legislature assigned the county enough land? To ensure Garfield's future, Eminence investor C. J. "Buffalo" Jones tried to add a strip from northern Gray County. Ravanna opposed this, and the idea failed.

The Garfield County Commission named Ravanna the temporary county seat until officials could hold an election. Bat Masterson and 20 deputies came from Dodge City to prevent election violence. Ravanna won, but Eminence refused to accept the results. Eventually, the state attorney general deducted 60 deceased Ravanna voters from the rolls, and Eminence became the county seat.

GHOSTLY GARFIELD COUNTY

WHAT: Finney County's "nose"

WHERE: Finney County Historical Society Museum, 403 S Fourth St., Garden City

COST: Donation

PRO TIP: Ravanna's ruins are at N Ravanna and E Lake Roads. The Eminence Cemetery is about a mile east of the N Ochs and E Eminence Roads intersection.

Ravanna officials refused to surrender the records, so Fred Smith and John Rader smuggled them out of the courthouse with Tom O'Toole and Michael Hainey in pursuit. Smith and Rader veered off the dark trail and hid in a draw. O'Toole and Hainey continued to Eminence, where L. W. Fulton locked them in a hotel room and rescued Smith and Rader.

Ravanna burned for revenge, arguing that Garfield County shouldn't be a county if Ravanna couldn't be the county seat. Ravanna's surveyor discovered that Garfield was four miles short of a legal county. The *Ravanna Chieftain* gloated, "Goodbye, Eminence, goodbye!" Garfield became Garfield Township, Finney County's nose.

However, the Kansas Pacific Railroad failed to build its promised spur from Ravanna to Dodge City. Without a railroad or a county seat nearby, the population crashed. Ravanna's obsession with revenge had killed both towns.

Officials in Leoti hired gunfighters, including Masterson, Wyatt Earp, and Doc Holliday, to intimidate voters choosing the Wichita County seat. Leoti won, and the opposing town of Coronado faded away. The hired guns posed for a photograph outside the Wichita County Bank. See the image at the Museum of the Great Plains, 201 N 4th St., Leoti 67861.

Ravanna ruins

A DEAD MAN FOR BREAKFAST

Where was Kansas's worst end-of-track town?

The towns at the end of railroad tracks were notorious for vice. The worst of all was Sheridan, east of McAllaster in Logan County. The Kansas Pacific Railroad ran out of funds when it reached Sheridan. The financial problems stranded 2,000 people in the end-of-track settlement from 1868 to 1870.

Life was cheap in Sheridan. Before a single street appeared, the surveyor had to build a graveyard. By the end of the first winter, 26 bodies inhabited the cemetery. Each month averaged four violent deaths. When the morning trains came into Sheridan, the engineers slowed so the passengers could view the trestle's freshly hanged bodies. People said Sheridan had a "dead man for breakfast every morning."

One of the residents went to bathe in the nearby pond— and stepped on a dead man's face. The body belonged to a gambler, and no one faced justice for his murder. Just another day in the Black Eye of Kansas.

The coroner was supposed to return any valuables to the decedents' families. Instead, the coroner became one of the wealthiest men in Sheridan. Some of the dead went to their graves without clothing, wrapped only in a blanket. Except for the graveyard, everything in Sheridan was temporary. The buildings rolled in on railroad cars. Saloons and their "soiled doves" (prostitutes) thrived, while railroaders and their families lived in shacks and dugouts in Rat Row. Many dwellings' only above-ground portions were the doors and the chimneys. The smoke that rose from the ground added to the hellish scene.

Home at Sheridan. Courtesy of DeGolyer Library/SMU

SHERIDAN

WHAT: Ghost town where the Kansas Pacific ran out of money

WHERE: North of Logan County Rte. 160 and Wagon Roads' intersection

COST: Free

PRO TIP: The house that sits below Consolation Points is private property, so please remain outside the fence.

Sheridan disappeared when the Kansas Pacific's tracks reached Kit Carson, Colorado, 80 miles west. The wicked town's only remains are the two buttes—called Consolation Points—and the streets. Kit Carson was never as wild as Sheridan because its most restless citizens remained behind forever.

Learn more about Sheridan at Fort Wallace Museum in Wallace. Fort Wallace surgeon Theophilus Turner discovered a large plesiosaur beside the buttes, and a replica hangs in the museum.

"NOBODY THERE NO HOW"

Where was Trail City?

Kansas banned "the manufacture and sale of intoxicating liquors" in 1881 and prohibited cattle drives three years later. The twin prohibitions formed Trail City's culture. In 1885, Martin Culver founded Trail City on Colorado's eastern edge. Since some of the town's saloons straddled the state line, the owners did not enforce Prohibition laws in the "Colorado rooms."

Cowboys entered Trail City's saloons on the Colorado side. After drinking, they threw their bottles out the back door into Kansas, saying, "Toss them into Kansas. There's nobody there no how."

Trail City is famous for many tragedies, but this one epitomizes the lawless life people lived on the border between Colorado and Kansas. I. P. "Print" Olive built a livery stable and a saloon, but he prohibited prostitutes from working in his place. His competitor Joe Sparrow added several rooms to his saloon where soiled doves imported from Dodge City worked. Sparrow owed Olive some money. And maybe Olive had lynched Sparrow's relative in Nebraska.

In December 1887, Olive tried to collect Sparrow's debt. "If you don't pay, I'll kill you," Olive said jokingly. Sparrow said he didn't have enough to eat. "Well, Joe, if that's the case, we'll say nothing more about it." Then Olive handed Sparrow enough money for a meal.

TRAIL CITY

WHAT: The last cow town

WHERE: 111 Elm St., Coolidge

COST: Free

PRO TIP: Trail City's remnants are on private property surrounding the Highway 400 and County Road 39 intersection west of Coolidge.

Trail City Bed & Breakfast. Courtesy of Trail City B&B

Meanwhile, Olive had quarreled with another man, John Stansfield. "If you kill [Olive], I'll stand by you," Stansfield told Sparrow. The two men ambushed the unarmed Olive. Sparrow's first shot wounded Olive, who cried, "My God, Joe, don't murder me!" Sparrow then shot Olive in the head. The Prowers County jury in Sparrow's first trial convicted him, but jury misconduct accusations forced a second trial in Pueblo, Colorado. The second jury acquitted him of the murder.

Trail City lasted for about three years. By 1890, settlers had fenced the land and removed the town's buildings.

In the 1983 film *National Lampoon's Vacation*, the Griswold family visited Cousin Eddie's Worm Farm set in Coolidge during their vacation trip across country. After the film became popular, a former Trail City saloon was converted to the Trail City Bed and Breakfast and Cousin Eddie's Visitor Center in 2014.

The Texas-Ogallala Trail left Kansas in Texas Trail Canyon. Ira Olive, Print's brother, killed Mexican Leon, one of the Olives' cowboys, there in the canyon in 1876. A marker on Highway 34, east of Haigler, Nebraska, tells the story.

NEVER RUNS DRY

Which natural spring has never run dry?

Fifteen miles south of Minneola, Clark County's geography dives into a hole. The Big Basin Overlook opens where Highway 283 bottoms out. It's not an overlook; it's a level look. The highway crosses the basin's floor for a mile before climbing 100 feet to escape. Several thousand years ago, a salt deposit dissolved hundreds of feet below the current basin's floor, causing it to collapse.

From the highway, search for a hill topped with a cairn. The cairn marks the way to the St. Jacob's Well in Little Basin, a spring that has never run dry. Wildlife and migrating people have come here over the years with their livestock. Sadly, hunters killed the last Clark County bison in 1874, but now an imported (and protected) herd inhabits the basins.

East of Big Basin, Little Basin's floor is about 280 yards wide with 35-foot-high walls. St. Jacob's Well is about 50 feet wide. Cowboys watered their cattle at the pool for decades. Traditionally, even after the water table has declined, the well does not run dry.

The area provides reasons to linger for a while, both scenic and historic. At the Highway 160 intersection south of the basins, turn east to Ashland. Stop at the Keiger Creek Bridge for excellent views of the Red Hills. Perhaps Lieutenant Colonel George Custer and Major Henry Inman

---

BIG BASIN AND ST. JACOB'S WELL

WHAT: A water source that never dries up

WHERE: Hwy. 283, Minneola

COST: Free

PRO TIP: Ashland's Clark County Courthouse exterior features an engraved stone map of the county's historic sites.

Cairn showing the way to St. Jacob's Well.

saw this same vista in 1868, when they explored a route from Fort Dodge to Camp Supply. When they climbed a 2,356-foot hill, Custer asked Inman its name. "It is Mount Jesus," Inman said.

Ten years later, the Northern Tsistsis'tas (Cheyenne) escaped their Oklahoma reservation and entered Clark County. Vóóhéhéve (Dull Knife) and his band camped in the Big Basin on September 10, 1878. They were trying to return home to Montana.

Final fun fact: although no county settlers died during the Last Indian Raid in Kansas, the H. T. Spencer Ranch in Clark and Comanche counties lost 132 of 650 head of cattle and J. H. Cruzen claimed $270 in crop losses.

The 300-acre Clark County State Fishing Lake looks more like a state park. Bluff Creek Canyon envelops the park, which offers camping, picnicking, and fishing.

NO BULL

Who killed Bull City?

Union Pacific Railroad officials encouraged Gen. Hiram Bull to start a town in the Solomon River Valley because the railroad intended to build there. On Bull's way west, he met Lyman T. Earl in Cawker City during the summer of 1870. Bull won a coin flip, and Osborne County's first town became Bull City.

The general developed a menagerie to amuse his daughter Nora and the community's other children. The animals included a large bull elk, which was so tame that the children fed it by hand. Then came the rut season. The elk seemed hostile when Robert Bricknell entered his pen to feed it on October 12, 1879. Bricknell and Bull picked up heavy clubs to subdue the animal. Instead, it attacked. George Nicholas and William Sherman rushed to help while Bull's wife, Sarah, watched. A notebook in his vest pocket saved Sherman from the worst of his injuries, but the others were gored to death. Sarah still wanted to keep the elk because it was a valuable animal, but the elk's aggression sealed its fate.

Two thousand people came to the triple funeral. The men's remains rest in Sumner Cemetery. A few years later, Sarah and Nora moved to Wisconsin.

Six years after the men's demise, Stella Clark decided that the name Bull City was vulgar. She claimed no one

ALTON

WHAT: The city that lost its name

WHERE: Alton City Park, Nicholas Ave. and Mill St.

COST: Free

PRO TIP: Candy magnate Russell Stover was born 10 miles south of Alton on County Road 657. A sign marks the spot.

would move to a town with such a nasty name. The citizens weren't interested in her concerns. When they petitioned for a new road, Clark surreptitiously pasted names from the road petition onto a name-change petition and submitted it to post office headquarters. Clark succeeded. The post office accepted the petition and changed Bull City's name to Alton, Clark's hometown, on April 1, 1885.

Clark and the elk combined to leave Bull City with no general, no elk, and a changed name. And that's no bull.

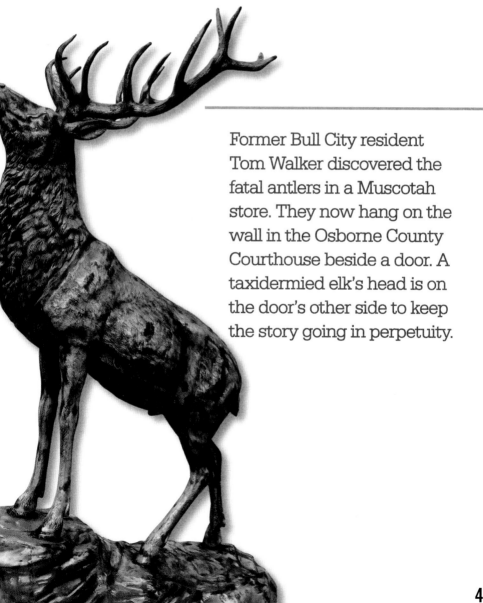

Former Bull City resident Tom Walker discovered the fatal antlers in a Muscotah store. They now hang on the wall in the Osborne County Courthouse beside a door. A taxidermied elk's head is on the door's other side to keep the story going in perpetuity.

A PLAGIARIZED PLEDGE

Who wrote the Pledge of Allegiance?

In 1890, the magazine *Youth's Companion* held a contest, a chance to create a Pledge of Allegiance. In Cherryvale, 13-year-old Frank E. Bellamy's teacher assigned the contest challenge as an essay. When the magazine's September 8, 1892, issue arrived, Bellamy saw his submission credited to Anonymous. The only difference: the magazine had substituted "indivisible" for "inseparable." When he questioned this, the magazine said all entries belonged to the magazine.

Francis J. Bellamy of the magazine's marketing staff claimed that he had composed the pledge on a "sultry August evening." He claimed that the pledge's opening words came quickly and that he then labored for two more hours before he finished: "I pledge allegiance to my Flag and the Republic for which it stands—one Nation indivisible—with liberty and justice for all." He later changed the wording to "and to the Republic."

Frank later submitted his composition to the Women's Relief Corps, a Civil War veterans' organization. His entry won while Frank was serving in the Spanish–American War. Unfortunately, Frank contracted tuberculosis during his service, and although he moved to Denver on his doctor's advice, he died there in 1915.

THE PLEDGE OF ALLEGIANCE'S KANSAS AUTHOR

WHAT: The Pledge of Allegiance's true author

WHERE: Frank Bellamy's remains rest in Cherryvale's Fairview Cemetery. The city dedicated a marker in Logan Park on Columbus Day 1996.

COST: Free

PRO TIP: Bellamy's marker is in the Cherryvale Veterans Memorial.

Courtesy Carol Staton, Cherryvale Museum

For many years, Francis Bellamy received credit for writing the pledge. Congress, the American Legion, the Smithsonian, and the US Flag Association credited him with its creation. Cherryvale residents protested, but to no avail.

Finally, Barry Popik, a New York historian, discovered an article from Victoria's *Ellis County News Republican*. It said students had recited the pledge on April 30, 1892, months before Francis said he had written it. Plus, the newspaper's quote included the word "inseparable." Popik's findings appeared in a *New York Times* article dated April 20, 2022. In it, Elizabeth L. Brown, a Library of Congress reference librarian, asks the pertinent question, "If Francis Bellamy wrote the pledge in August of 1892, how did it come to be published in Kansas . . . in May 1892?" Based on these findings, Frank E. Bellamy of Cherryvale, was the original author of the Pledge of Allegiance.

The Pledge of Allegiance received its final form on Flag Day 1954 when fellow Kansan Dwight D. Eisenhower signed Public Law 396. The law added "under God" after "one Nation" to the final version of the Pledge.

DOROTHY GALE'S INSPIRATION

Did L. Frank Baum's Dorothy Gale live in Irving?

The book *Storm Kings: America's First Tornado Chasers* claims that a Kansas tornado victim inspired L. Frank Baum's Dorothy in *The Wonderful Wizard of Oz*. According to the author, Baum's inspiration drowned in a puddle after an 1879 Irving storm.

May 30, 1879, was oppressive and hot. People in Irving, a small town in southern Marshall County, expected a storm. Instead, at about 4 p.m., a funnel cloud approached Irving from the southwest and destroyed three homes. Another twister came from the northwest about 20 minutes later, collapsing at least 10 buildings. Then they joined and created a devastating tornado that pelted the ruined town with hailstones eight inches in diameter. For some reason, the F-5 storm had chosen Irving for its epicenter, nearly obliterating the town.

The *Blue Rapids Times* listed 11 dead in Irving with many injured, but more communities had suffered, too.

The regional death toll stood at 66. The Signals Service sent Pvt. J. P. Finley to investigate. He interviewed the victims and witnesses, examined the storm tracks, and checked the damage. In his detailed 116-page report, he mentioned the John Gail family. But Finley was a poor speller and often misspelled names: "Gail" became "Gale."

According to Finley's report, the tornado struck the Gails' home first. The twister carried baby Nellie 500 feet into a ravine, and her sister Alta Gail landed nearby. The storm dropped their parents 165 to 250 feet away from their ruined home. All of them survived. None of them were named Dorothy.

A few blocks away, the twister overturned the Kenneys' house. Three adults died, including Flora. Rescuers found her naked body with her head buried up to her shoulders. Kenney's fate sounds like the Wicked Witch of the East's demise in the Oz story.

Most scholars believe that Baum named Dorothy for his deceased niece Dorothy Gage. But maybe the Irving victims inspired her last name and the background circumstances of her fantastic adventure.

IRVING

WHAT: The tornado that might have inspired Oz

WHERE: Blue Rapids Museum, 36 Public Sq., Blue Rapids

COST: Donation

PRO TIP: Irving's marker stands at 12th and Zenith Roads near Blue Rapids. Look for its foundations on both sides of the road south of the monument. Please remain within the right of way.

Because of the Great Flood of 1951, the Bureau of Reclamation removed Irving's citizens to make way for Tuttle Creek Lake. A concrete marker denotes its location.

"NEVER TAKE NO CUTOFFS"

Would we know about the Donner Party if Sarah Keyes had lived?

Consumption (tuberculosis) ravaged Sarah Keyes's body and her doctors told Sarah that she wouldn't live much longer. She wanted to see her son again, but he had moved to California. Her family sent word to Robert Keyes: meet us at Fort Hall in southeastern Idaho.

Her daughter Margret and son-in-law John Frazier Reed built a special wagon to transport Keyes to the meeting place. The Jacob and George Donner families joined the Reeds. They started west on the Oregon–California Trail from Independence, Missouri, on May 12, 1846–a month later than they had planned. The success of such trips relied heavily on leaving before snow fell in the mountains.

Most groups embarked on the journey in mid-April so that by mid-May, the wagon would pass Fort Kearny, near present-day Kearney, Nebraska. Mid-June should see Fort Laramie, and South Pass, Wyoming, was the Independence Day goal. To avoid the severe Sierra Nevada winters, emigrants needed to cross the mountains by mid-September.

ALCOVE SPRING

WHAT: The start of the Donner Party disaster

WHERE: Alcove Spring Historic Park. From Blue Rapids, take Highway 77 north to Schroyer Rd. Look for a sign just before the Georgia-Pacific gypsum mine. Follow the road 5 miles north to the park. Avoid the road in wet weather.

COST: Free

PRO TIP: Sarah Keyes's marker is across from the parking lot. Also, look for wagon swales, the depressions the heavily laden wagons carved into the ground.

Two weeks after they left Independence, the Donners reached the Big Blue River crossing between present-day Blue Rapids and Marysville. The flooded river stranded them from May 26 to May 31. While they were waiting, Edwin Bryant discovered and named Alcove Spring where the pure, ice-cold water dropped 10 or 12 feet.

On May 29, Keyes died. After her death, the party no longer needed to visit Fort Hall so they pushed on for the Hastings Cutoff—a "shortcut" that had never been successfully tried. It became a month-long disaster. However, despite all their delays, they still could have gotten through with one last push. Instead, they rested, and the snow stranded the Donner-Reed party in a notorious nightmare of starvation and death. Almost half of them died. Their horrific story depressed California travel until the Gold Rush. If Keyes had lived, the party would have avoided their disastrous shortcut. A less eventful journey would have made them anonymous.

Even after her trials, survivor Virginia Reed wrote, "Don't let this letter dishearten anybody and never take no cutoffs and hurry along as fast as you can."

Several pioneer travelers autographed the rocks around Alcove Spring. John Reed carved his initials and date above the falls, as did explorer John C. Fremont.

FOOLHARDY FREIGHTERS AND A THRESHING MACHINE

Why would freighters camp in such a vulnerable place?

John C. Fremont blazed the Smoky Hill Trail through what later became Threshing Machine Canyon in 1844. T.R. Hunt of New Jersey carved his name in the 75-foot bluff five years later. Hunt set a precedent for leaving graffiti, and for years people's names covered the bluff, canyon walls, and fallen boulders. One Missourian even engraved his name and the unlikely date of 10 B.C.

In the meantime, the Smoky Hill Trail became notorious as an ambush site. The Tsistsis'tas (Cheyenne) and Hinono'eiteen (Arapaho) tribes resented those who traveled through their hunting grounds, driving off the game. The Native Americans had observed that where White people traveled, they eventually settled, and the raiders were determined that such settling would not happen. Besides, raiding was profitable.

In 1867, a group of warriors spotted freight wagons carrying a threshing machine, used for separating grain from stalks, reputedly bound for Brigham Young's Salt Lake City. The heavy machine slowed the train, and the warriors

THRESHING MACHINE CANYON

WHAT: Freighters become targets

WHERE: Bluffton Area, Cedar Bluff State Park, Hwy. 147 and West Rd.

COST: Kansas state park permit

PRO TIP: Camp at the state park's Despatch Campground across from the canyon.

easily followed. Wise Plains travelers camped away from potential ambush sites, but these freighters had not learned that lesson. Instead, they camped beside a high bluff across from a ravine.

When the freighters went to bed, the warriors crawled down the ravine. They killed and scalped the freighters and then, in contempt, they burned the machine. The tragedy gave the canyon its name.

The burned machine stayed at the bluff's base, and souvenir hunters hauled away the pieces. Machine parts littered Threshing Machine Canyon for years. Eventually, bluff chunks and wind-blown dirt buried the site, and a weed thicket covered it.

The canyon now anchors the Cedar Bluff Wildlife Area. The canyon's trail is now closed, but take Cedar Bluff State Park's 1.25-mile Butterfield Hiking Trail to learn more.

Threshing Machine Canyon. Courtesy of WaKeeney Travel & Tourism

The Trego County Historical Museum in WaKeeney preserves the remaining machine parts.

THE GAS THAT REFUSED TO BURN

What was Dexter's "wind gas?"

Visions of prosperity danced in Dexter citizens' heads in 1903. Nine million cubic feet of gas each day escaped from a "howling gasser" of a well. The people decided to inaugurate the well with a festival. Their flyers promised, "A great pillar of flame from the burning well will light the entire countryside for a day and a night."

At the festival's climax, the mayor brought a burning hay bale to the well. The roaring gas extinguished the flames. He tried several times, but the gas still would not burn. The disappointed crowd dispersed, grumbling about the "wind gas" and the "well of hot air."

The officials of Dexter felt dismayed, but the state geologist, Erasmus Haworth, was intrigued. He ordered a large cylinder filled with the mysterious gas. When Haworth returned to Lawrence, his and David McFarland's analysis showed the gas contained nitrogen, methane, and an "inert residue."

McFarland and fellow chemist Hamilton Cady distilled the gas, and their spectroscope showed helium. They devised a method to isolate helium. However, no one knew what to do with it. Later, University of Kansas graduate student Clifford Siebel presented a paper in Kansas

---

DEXTER HELIUM PARK

WHAT: Helium discovered on earth

WHERE: Valley Ave. and N Main St. intersection, Dexter

COST: Free

PRO TIP: Henry family legend says Tom Henry invented the Oh Henry bar, and Mama Henry bars are handmade at Henry's Candies, 21172 Hwy. 15, Dexter.

Helium Park
Dexter, Kansas
Where Helium was Discovered

City, regretting that helium had no uses. A Bureau of Mines representative then read a letter from Nobel Prize Laureate Sir William Ramsay. The letter asked the Americans to continue to produce helium, because Ramsay claimed that helium had almost the same lift as hydrogen without flammable hydrogen's dangers.

Dexter gained a helium plant in 1927 that supplied navy dirigibles. Although the Americans could not increase helium production fast enough for World War I, navy blimps escorted ships across the ocean during World War II, kept afloat by this marvelous nonflammable gas. In the 1950s, the plant flourished when demand soared for helium in nuclear reactors and missiles. Sadly, the Dexter field no longer produces helium.

Cady and McFarland isolated the helium in Bailey Hall. For its role in isolating the element, the American Chemical Society named Bailey Hall a National Historical Chemical Landmark in 2000. The hall's namesake, Dr. E. H. S. Bailey, created University of Kansas's Rock Chalk Jayhawk cheer.

FINDING BLACK GOLD

How did El Dorado help win World War I?

El Dorado means "golden land" in Spanish, but its citizens weren't feeling very golden in the early 1900s. Neighboring Augusta had found natural gas, but El Dorado had found nothing. They had even hired a spiritualist, to no avail.

Augusta's success inspired El Dorado to hire Erasmus Haworth, who was about to retire as the state geologist. He discovered the El Dorado Anticline (uplift). Because oil is lighter than water, it moves upward. When impermeable rock seals the anticline, the oil is trapped. As a result, an oil-rich reservoir forms.

The city leased 790 acres, but its first well was dry. Wichita Natural Gas Co. purchased El Dorado's drilling rights a month later. Within a week, Stapleton Well No. 1 struck black gold at 2,497 feet. The Kansas oil boom was on.

Warren Martin of Kansas Oil and Natural Gas Producers quipped that before 1915, oil companies saw geologists as being "in the same vein as witching and doodlebugs." The discovery of the El Dorado well turned geology into "one of the great science industries." Stapleton's success encouraged other companies and, as a result, El Dorado's population soared. Eventually, the Empire Gas & Fuel Company built Oil Hill, a 64-acre company town northwest of El Dorado.

By 1918, El Dorado led the nation in oil production. It produced nearly nine million barrels of oil, almost 9 percent

---

KANSAS OIL MUSEUM

WHAT: The first use of geology to find oil

WHERE: 383 E Central Ave., El Dorado

COST: Donation

PRO TIP: Visit the Stapleton No. 1 Oil Well at NW Rocky and NW Boyer Rds. during daylight hours.

of the nation's oil output. El Dorado's output was crucial to the war effort because the British and American navies burned oil. Their armies used over 100,000 motorized vehicles and thousands of airplanes. Oil tanker losses in the Atlantic caused dire shortages. The shortfall was so bad that the Allies considered switching to coal.

US convoys staved off the shortfall. Future British Foreign Secretary Lord George Curzon said, "The Allied cause had floated to victory on a wave of oil." Since then, the oil field has produced nearly three billion barrels.

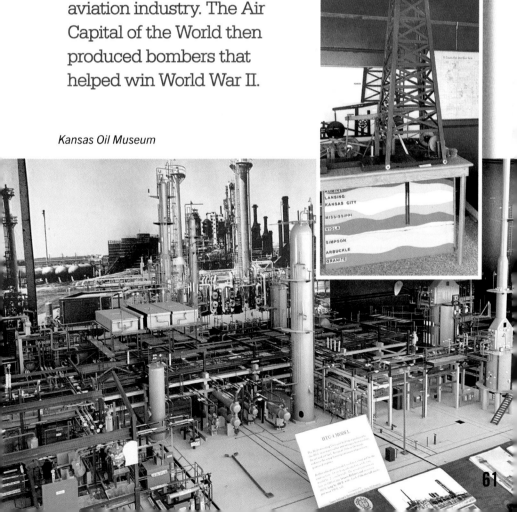

Some of El Dorado's oil tycoons invested in Wichita's aviation industry. The Air Capital of the World then produced bombers that helped win World War II.

Kansas Oil Museum

MAESTRO SEMICONDUCTOR

What if Jack Kilby had gone on vacation in 1958?

Texas Instruments (TI) required employees to take a two-week vacation every July. However, Jack Kilby hadn't yet earned time off. While everyone else was away on break, Kilby began playing with integrated circuits. On September 12, 1958, Kilby successfully demonstrated the first microchip.

Up until then, computer engineering had faced the "tyranny of numbers." The more complex the device, the more components it requires. And the parts had to be assembled by hand. Every joint formed a potential weak point.

Alone in a cavernous building, Kilby experienced a eureka moment. He sketched "the Monolithic Idea" into his lab notebook. TI could make all the circuit elements, a transistor, a capacitor, and a bulk resistor from the same block on a single chip. His integrated circuit was a thin germanium slice with one bipolar transistor, four input/output terminals, and gold wires. His device was half the size of a paper clip. After he invented the integrated circuit, devices that had previously required a room shrank to pocket size.

On Demonstration Day, Kilby hooked an oscilloscope to his

JACK KILBY

WHAT: The semiconductor's inventor

WHERE: Barton County Historical Museum, 85 S Hwy. 281; Jack Kilby Plaza, 1400 Main St., Great Bend

COST: Donation

PRO TIP: About the same time as Kilby's invention, Robert Noyce of Fairchild Industries also devised an integrated circuit. Eventually, the companies cross-licensed their inventions.

wafer. Then, as the executives watched, he turned on the power, and a sine wave appeared on the screen.

When Kilby attended Great Bend High, his father worked for an electric company. When a storm knocked out power, his dad communicated with ham radio operators to track power outages. This incident sparked Kilby's interest in electronics. After he earned his bachelor's and master's degrees in electrical engineering, Kilby moved to Dallas. He had chosen TI because the company promised to let him work on electric component miniaturization full-time. TI's decision paid off for the company.

The circuit became integral to modern technology. Without Kilby's miniaturization, Apollo 11 would not have flown, the Internet would not exist, and cords would still tie phones to walls. In 2000, Kilby received the Nobel Prize in Physics.

Kilby and coworkers Jerry Merryman and James van Tassel invented the first handheld calculators because TI needed people to see the integrated circuit's benefits.

CAN YOU HEAR ME NOW?

What if Cleyson Brown had become a farmer?

Cleyson Brown established Brown Telephone Company in Abilene five years after Alexander Graham Bell's patents expired. Eventually, his company became a global telecommunications giant.

Brown's father, Jacob, owned a grist mill south of Abilene. When the boy was nine, a power corn sheller crushed his arm between the cogs. Doctors had to amputate the damaged limb. He used a prosthetic arm and hand for the rest of his life. Without that accident, Brown would probably have become a farmer.

Instead, father and son started an electric company in 1898. The grist mill generated the power. The power company was successful, and Brown began the telephone company four years later. When power poles and lines began cluttering Abilene's landscape, Brown decided to bury the lines. In 1911, he changed Brown Telephone's name to United Telephone Company.

As Brown's business ventures expanded, so did his profits. One-quarter of Abilene's families depended on his companies. He believed saving boosted success and mandated that his employees invest 10 percent of their earnings. Many of them invested in Brown's enterprises. Then David Eisenhower, future president Dwight Eisenhower's father, became the savings committee's secretary.

Brown and his sisters Jennie and Della formed the Brown Memorial Foundation in 1926. By 1930, it had given over a million dollars to Abilene causes. Brown Memorial Park held 226 acres, a zoo, a golf course, and an amusement park. Its operating costs required $1,000 per day but charged no admission.

Then the Great Depression wiped out Brown's fortune. He died bankrupt on November 12, 1935. However, Brown's legacy lives on at Brown Memorial Home for the Aged and Brown Memorial Park. Boy Scouts camp on 40 acres of that park. His telephone corporation became Sprint in 1982, and Sprint merged with T-Mobile in 2020. Kansas City Power & Light bought Brown's power company. It's now Evergy.

CLEYSON (C. L.) BROWN

WHAT: Starting a global telecommunications giant

WHERE: Museum of Independent Telephony, Heritage Center of Dickinson County, 412 S Campbell St., Abilene

COST: $8 for adults 15–61; $7 for adults 62 and older; $4 for children from 2–14

PRO TIP: Ride the world's oldest C. W. Parker Carousel in the museum complex. It's hand-carved with 24 horses and four chariots. Adults older than 14 pay $4 per ride. Children's admission fees include a ride for free.

When business suddenly dropped at Almon Strowger's Kansas City, Missouri, funeral home in 1878, Strowger discovered that the central telephone operator was routing all of his calls to the operator's husband's business. Strowger got even by inventing direct-dial calling. See how it worked at the Museum of Independent Telephony.

INSPIRATION FROM A NOTEBOOK

How did a pocket notebook fuel Walter Chrysler's success?

Walter Chrysler's first job was delivering milk produced by his mother's cows. By the end of his life, Chrysler owned one of the world's largest automotive companies.

Every day, the boy carried milk to his customers for a nickel per quart. He recorded each purchase in a pocket notebook and collected each payday. The boy desired to become a railroad machinist. His father refused to allow it. Instead, the younger Chrysler swept the railroad shop's floors. Six months later, he became an apprentice.

Apprentices had to craft their own tools, including depth gauges. Most gauges measured tolerances to a one-eighth inch, but Chrysler's measured one-sixteenth inch. Later, when he became wealthy, Chrysler displayed his tools and toolbox on the Chrysler Building's top floor. He wrote everything in his notebooks as he continued to rise. Meanwhile, his childhood sweetheart Della Forker waited five years to marry him on June 6, 1901.

In 1912, Chrysler began managing Buick, a car company that was losing money. Buick officials did not understand the company's costs. Its test drivers stole cars. Chrysler kept his detailed notes and as a result, Buick soon turned massive profits.

Eventually he started his own company. Chrysler Corporation bought Dodge Brothers in 1928. With its Plymouth line, Chrysler challenged Ford Corporation and General Motors' Chevrolet on the low-end car market. In a year, he had pushed the auto industry from the Big Two to the Big Three. *Time* named him Man of the Year.

Finally, on October 16, he announced the construction of the Chrysler Building, which would become the world's tallest structure. The workers hid the Chrysler Building's spire until the end to ensure a world record in 1930. The Empire State Building set a new standard the following year, but the Chrysler made more money.

Chrysler retired in 1935 but remained chairman of the board until he died on August 18, 1940. The pocket notebook always went with him wherever he went.

WALTER P. CHRYSLER

WHAT: The rise of an automobile magnate

WHERE: Chrysler Boyhood Home, 102 W 10th St., Ellis

COST: $2 for children 6–11, $4 for children 12–adult, $3 for seniors 65 and over

PRO TIP: Elias Disney, Walt Disney's father, worked with Chrysler in the Ellis railroad shops. Elias eventually left Ellis, but the family buried the elder Disneys in Mount Hope Cemetery in Ellis. Della Chrysler's parents also rest there.

Chrysler's Redstone rocket powered Alan Shepard's Freedom 7 and Gus Grissom's Liberty Bell 7. Its Saturn 1B pushed Apollo 7 into space. The Apollo 11 crew—Neil Armstrong, Buzz Aldrin, and Michael Collins—rode through a New York ticker-tape parade in a Chrysler Imperial Parade Phaeton.

CHROME-PLATED DREAMS

Where is the Kustom Kemps Hall of Fame?

Museum association president Tom Pestinger was driving around with some friends in 2014. "Jokingly, I said, 'Why don't we build a car museum?'" The Garage opened on February 20, 2022.

If you think the Garage in Salina will be one of those overstuffed car museums, think again. This museum allows maximum hands-on participation. If you're escorting children, turn left and pass through the gift shop. Immediately, here come the Hot Wheels, and over there is a pinewood derby track. Oh, and don't miss the bin full of Lego building blocks. A cool racing video game is over there. Oh, my! If you aren't itching to play, something's wrong. Let's not be rude or pushy, adults, but this is too much fun to let the kids enjoy everything.

The Garage offers a lounge library if you insist on letting only the kids play with the toys, but seriously, don't miss the Standard Oil station where you can try your hand at virtual welding and painting inside. If you can tear yourself away from the toys, explore the Kustom Kemps Hall

---

THE GARAGE

WHAT: Salina car museum

WHERE: 134 S 4th St., Salina

COST: $15 for adults. Seniors, military, and students are $12. Children under three are free.

PRO TIP: If you're not escorting children, turn right at the entrance toward the snack bar. Pour a cold brew from one of the taps and buy a snack.

of Fame (so named because teens in the late 1950s to early '60s called automobiles "kemps"). The exhibits rotate every six months, so visit often.

Check out the Andy Warhol–style Elvis mural. Both of them would probably drool over the sweet rides. The official selfie station nearby, a car bench in front of a vintage Santa Fe Avenue streetscape, awaits you.

The Crossroads Car Experience houses classic cars. Some of them slowly spin on giant turntables. Play trivia and gas pump games. Some walls showcase classic neon and Kansas road trip images while vintage hubcaps cover one whole wall.

You'd better start driving to the Garage because your inner child is saying, "Are we there yet?"

Kustom Kemps of America (KKOA) holds a show in Salina each July. KKOA is America's oldest and largest custom car and truck association.

NOSTALGIA AT THE PUMP

Which city is the Vintage Gas Station Capital?

Start your Norton nostalgic service station tour at the Norton Business & Visitor Station at 205 South State Street, a former Kent Oil Company service station donated by Roger and Michael Moffet. A crew of volunteers renovated it as an office space, finishing it in 2011. Three such stations are within easy walking distance of each other.

Larry Urban has restored his classic Conoco service station with vintage pumps, oil cans, maps, a chest freezer 7Up pop machine, and a Ford Galaxie on the station's service bay rack. (The rack is a replacement.) If you feel like channeling Clark Kent, step into the telephone booth for your Superman moment.

The station at 110 South First also features an early oil pump. Early drivers didn't have plastic bottles of oil in their trunks. Instead, the service station's staff would pump the oil into glass bottles with a hand-cranked pump. When a driver asked for an oil check, the attendant filled the car's oil reservoir if needed.

The Sinclair service station at 119 South First and the adjoining Scheetz Motor Company building were in sad shape. Mick and Colette Miller took pity on the battered buildings and began restoring them to their former glory. Dino the dinosaur mascot again stands proudly on top of the service station. The Millers restored the motor company signs to their initial appearance. Sinclair's signature dinosaur and the signs proclaim, "We're back!"

Dinosaurs have been Sinclair's trademark since the 1930s. Sinclair's marketers named their dinosaur Dino (DYE-no). Sinclair's Apatosaurus became such a hit that Sinclair trademarked him in 1932. Fiberglass Dinos came to local Sinclair stations in the early 1960s, and they have been popular ever since.

When you call for tours, ask to also see Goof's Big Boy's Toys Museum.

THE PLANET HUNTER

What if Clyde Tombaugh had gone straight to college?

A severe hailstorm destroyed the crops on Clyde Tombaugh's farm. Because of the damage, Tombaugh could not attend college. Would he have discovered Pluto as a college student?

Before graduating high school in 1925, Tombaugh was already a skilled amateur astronomer. However, his Sears telescope did not impress him. Instead, he built an eight-inch reflector from boards and farm equipment. He was still dissatisfied, so he hand-dug a hole to create a laboratory. In 1928, he crafted a nine-inch reflector from a Buick crankshaft and cream separator parts. Then he started sketching Jupiter and Mars. Eventually, he sent his detailed observations to Lowell Observatory for critique. Instead, the observatory offered him a job. His mission was to search for a mysterious planet with their new telescope.

When William Herschel discovered Uranus in 1781, the planet's orbit didn't fit Isaac Newton's laws. Neptune's discovery in 1846 solved some, but not all, of the issues. Astronomers speculated that another planet had to exist. Lowell Observatory founder Percival Lowell became obsessed with finding the disruptive unknown world, but he died before its discovery.

The Lowell telescope photographed pairs of images on different days. A blink compactor flipped between the photographs, using the principle that planets moved while

CLYDE TOMBAUGH

WHAT: Pluto's discoverer

WHERE: Marker at Hwy. 156 and Maple St., Burdett

COST: Free

PRO TIP: Play miniature golf at Burdett's Rediscover Pluto Miniature Golf Course in City Park, Michigan Ave. and Locust St.

Voyager Terra

Hayabusa Terra

Djanggawul Fossae

Al-Idrisi Montes

Burney

Sputnik Planitia

Sleipnir Fossae

Tartarus

Dorsa

Hillary Montes

Tenzing Montes

Adlivun Cavus

Tombaugh Regio

Pluto feature names NASA-APL-SwRI. Inset: Tombaugh with his homemade telescope. Courtesy of NASA

stars were stationary. Tombaugh studied these pairs for a week. Each set contained at least 150,000 stars to nearly a million. At 4 p.m. on February 18, 1930, Tombaugh saw movement in a pair photographed on January 21. Conditions were "the worst seeing in my life." Wind vibration had swollen Pluto's image, but it was visible. The observatory confirmed his work and announced the ninth planet on March 13.

The University of Kansas provided Pluto's discoverer with a scholarship. He earned degrees from KU and Northern Arizona University and continued his discoveries. The asteroid 1604 Tombaugh bears his name, as does a heart-shaped region on Pluto.

NASA's New Horizons project left Earth on January 19, 2006. The spacecraft carried some of Tombaugh's ashes past the dwarf planet on July 14, 2015. In a twist of fate, New Horizons Project Manager Glen Fountain grew up in Arlington, an hour and a half southeast of Burdett.

FLY ME TO THE MOON

Which Kansan lived closest to the stars?

The Kansas motto is *Ad Astra per Aspera*—"to the stars through difficulties." Ron Evans, Apollo 17's Command Module Pilot, orbited the moon for a record 147 hours, 43 minutes. While Evans orbited alone, his Apollo 17 crewmates, Eugene Cernan and Harrison (Jack) Schmitt, explored Mare Serenitatis, the Man in the Moon's left eye.

"I'd like to get down to the moon's surface," Evans said. "But there's a . . . lot of compensation [with flying] 240,000 miles away from earth."

Evans was born in St. Francis on November 30, 1933, and attended school in St. Francis and Topeka. He graduated from the University of Kansas in 1955 and received his commission as an ensign. He flew over 100 combat missions over Vietnam from the USS *Ticonderoga*. NASA accepted Evans as an astronaut in 1966. For the next six years, Evans supported Apollo missions, including Apollo 7, Apollo 11, and Apollo 14. He routinely dressed in patriotic colors during media appearances with a sunflower lapel pin. The media nicknamed him "Captain America."

Finally, Evans got his chance. Apollo 17's December 1972 trip toward the stars was not without difficulties. Terrorists threatened the astronaut's families. Only 30 seconds before liftoff, a fuel tank issue delayed the flight for three hours.

RON EVANS

WHAT: Record-setting astronaut

WHERE: Museum of Cheyenne County, W Hwy. 36, St. Francis

COST: Donation

PRO TIP: Evans presented a plaque that hangs in the Ron Evans Apollo Room in Nichols Hall. In addition, the Kenneth Spencer Research Library owns a moon rock from Apollo 17's record haul.

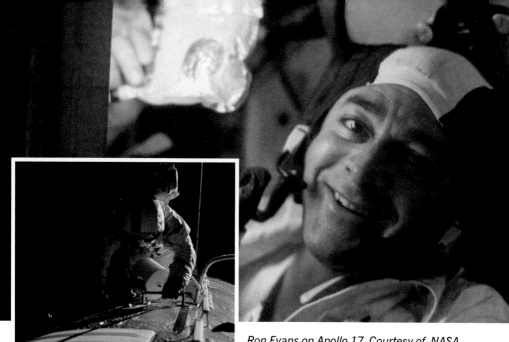

Ron Evans on Apollo 17. Courtesy of NASA

While his crewmates were on the moon, Evans flew the command module *America* and mapped the lunar surface. After he completed those tasks, he spacewalked for 47 minutes to retrieve the film. "Hot diggety dog!" he exclaimed when he stepped outside.

When *America* splashed down after a world record 301 hours, 51 minutes in space, Evans's former ship, the *Ticonderoga*, rescued them. Sadly, Apollo 17 held the last lunar visitors.

KU almost had two alumni aboard Apollo 17. Chapman's Joe Engel was supposed to be the Lunar Module Pilot, but was bumped when geologist Schmitt joined Apollo 17. Engel later commanded *Columbia* and *Discovery* space shuttle flights. Salina's Steve Hawley also flew in shuttles, while Hoxie's Nick Hague lived aboard the International Space Station.

THE DREAM THAT FAILED TO FLY

Who invented America's first patented helicopter?

In downtown Goodland, a painted helicopter flies above a sunflower field on the side of an old grocery store. Unfortunately, the helicopter it depicts never flew under its own power.

In fact, the helicopter's initial flight existed solely in Mrs. A. D. McIntyre's imagination. However, her flight of imagination inspired the craft's inventor, William Purvis. His device had yet to fly, but perhaps one last try would work. He strapped the flying machine to a threshing machine and climbed aboard. Then he crashed into the town water tank. He drenched himself and his spectators. The machine lay in pieces.

Purvis's dream was in pieces, too.

A year earlier, children playing with a whirligig inspired him to create a helicopter. He recruited his friend Charles A. "Art" Wilson to help. The railroad mechanics built a 400-pound prototype. Two sets of helicopter blades on two shafts spanned 18 feet.

Goodland Aviation Company scheduled a Thanksgiving Day demonstration. The whole town came. The demonstration impressed the audience, and people flocked to invest.

AMERICA'S FIRST PATENTED HELICOPTER

WHAT: The helicopter that never got off the ground

WHERE: High Plains Museum, 1717 Cherry Ave., Goodland

COST: Donation

PRO TIP: In Girard, Henry Laurens Call tinkered with aircraft design. The citizens dubbed the first design the Call Mayfly, as in "it may fly." It didn't. The Girard History Museum tells the story.

The inventors filed for a patent on March 18, 1910. In the next month, they bought a shop and machinery. The unmanned copter could fly several feet into the air when the conditions were right. However, the motors were too weak. Purvis went to St. Louis for a larger engine. He didn't find a motor and his partner moved to Kansas City.

After the tank disaster, the investors asked Purvis to install a propeller. Perhaps a propeller would combat the helicopter's top-heaviness and torque issues. He refused.

If Purvis had listened, perhaps Goodland Aviation would have soared. In 1939, Igor Sikorsky added a vertical rotor (or propeller) to his invention. The propeller solved the torque issue.

Two months after Mrs. McIntyre's vision, Purvis and his family moved to Missouri. Their investors auctioned the company assets. Two months later, the US Patent Office approved Goodland Aviation's application.

Harold Norton of Brewster built a replica of the helicopter for the High Plains Museum. With more capital, Purvis probably would have solved the aircraft's issues, Norton said. Visitors can turn the replica's rotors with a push of a button.

AMELIA AND *MURIEL*

Who owns the last Lockheed Electra 10-E?

Amelia Earhart, Atchison's most famous resident, visited her hometown during the Kansas Editors Convention on June 8, 1935. Atchison citizens crowded the parade route to see their aviation heroine. Unfortunately, she disappeared into the Pacific Ocean two years later. Navigator Fred Noonan and their Lockheed Electra 10-E vanished with her.

Nearly 80 years later, Atchison residents lined the streets again in Earhart's honor. This time the airplane *Muriel* was the guest. She was on her way to her new home in the Amelia Earhart Hangar Museum. *Muriel*'s specially built hangar had been attached to the Atchison Municipal Airport terminal. *Muriel* is the last remaining Lockheed Electra 10-E, the same model Earhart flew to her mysterious end. Amelia's sister, Grace Muriel Earhart Morrissey, preserved the aviator's legacy.

The gleaming aircraft is the museum's centerpiece. In work stations placed strategically around the plane, guests can try riveting, explore engine design, fly in a simulator, or prepare for takeoff.

The airplane traveled the world before it arrived in Atchison. *Muriel* began her life in 1935 when she flew between Brazil and Argentina for Pan American Airlines. In the 1950s, she flew between New England and New York. In 1970, the plane went to Florida. She endured two decades of torture, first as a skydiving plane and then as an outdoor museum exhibit in extreme heat and humidity. *Muriel* barely escaped the scrapyard.

However, Grace McGuire wanted a 10-E. She rescued the battered plane, named it *Muriel*, and spent 30 years restoring it to replicate the vanished plane. McGuire hoped

The airplane Muriel

to copy Amelia's final flight, but her health prevented her. Instead, she sold her plane to the hangar museum. The museum did not want to risk flying *Muriel* cross-country, so the dismantled plane rode on a truck bed for 1,206 miles from Southern California to Atchison. Her journey began on Amelia's 119th birthday.

On July 27, 2022, House Speaker Nancy Pelosi unveiled Amelia's statue in the US Capitol with museum board members at hand. The Kansas Legislature had voted to enshrine Amelia in 1999, but fundraising, sculpting, and COVID-19 delayed the event. A replica statute stands before the hangar museum's entrance.

TOUCH DOWN AT THE BEAUMONT HOTEL

Where can you fly to a hotel?

Whether you fly or drive, you'll love the Beaumont Hotel RV Park in Beaumont. The tiny town of 36 people is an oasis. If you're driving, Beaumont is less than an hour from Wichita on Highway 400. From March to October, the hotel hosts Biker Weekends each third Sunday.

But flying in is faster. What could be more convenient for aviation than crossing the airstrip to your hotel? The hotel holds Fly-in Weekends from Wednesdays through Sundays. Before making the trip, check the Beaumont AirNav information.

The first man to fly into Beaumont came in 1948. A cattle baron desired to fly in to check his livestock. The citizens blocked Main Street for his landing, and soon the word spread. Residents soon learned to watch for planes while driving. Five years later, the hotel owner built a landing strip east of the hotel. A Twin Beech stands beside the runway's end.

A FLY-IN HOTEL

WHAT: Beaumont Hotel RV Park

WHERE: 11651 SE Main St., Beaumont

COST: Depends on room size or RV hookup

PRO TIP: To avoid a plane-car collision, watch for the signs designating the airstrip and the street.

The word spread about the fly-in hotel. Five years later, Clint Squier remodeled the hotel so that when Texas cattlemen visited him, they would stay right on site. Their cowboys camped outside. Squier removed the fence between the hotel and the airstrip in 1962. Much later, in

AIRCRAFT ONLY BEYOND THIS POINT

Airplane and Frisco water tower

2001, Stephen Craig began to restore the hotel to its 1950s appearance. The quaint café is a throwback to that era.

Beaumont only covers a few blocks, so exploring is easy. First, walk to the Fresnos water retention ponds south of the hotel. Then visit the restored Beaumont Depot, the historic Frisco water tower, and the Twin Beech airplane. The lawn between the hotel and the RV park holds a unique version of the horseshoes game. Instead of poles, aim for cones.

Over the years, some people claimed to have encountered the ghost of a murdered cowboy. Room 201 is the one most often haunted; the spirit seems to like playing with clock radios.

THE MAN WHO SAVED THE MAIL

Which pilot lost his life but preserved the mail?

In the 1920s, pilots flirted with death every time they flew. Clarence Audburn Gilbert of Plainville lost his gamble on December 21, 1924. He was the first airmail pilot to die after the post office had started night flying only five months before.

Gilbert was no rookie. He had flown for the army during World War I. He left Maywood, Illinois, at 7 p.m. with a cargo of Christmas mail. His route went to Iowa City and on to Omaha. Snow was already flying; his hands and feet were frostbitten. Gilbert was tired because he had already flown earlier that day.

R. L. Wagner took off five minutes after Gilbert. Forty miles later, Wagner saw navigation lights near Kaneville, Illinois. Gilbert was either flying very low or was on the ground. The airmail service had an emergency field 17 miles west of Kaneville, but Gilbert didn't make it. For some reason, he strapped on his parachute and cut the engine. Then he stepped out into the storm.

Everything went wrong. Gilbert's parachute snagged on the tail, which severed the chute's lines, rendering it useless. Gilbert plummeted to earth. The plane crashed a mile north of Kaneville but didn't burn. The mail was safe because Gilbert had switched off the ignition. When Wagner arrived in Iowa City, he asked about Gilbert. After 15 hours, citizens found the missing pilot in a snow drift. A piece of his damaged parachute hung from his belt.

R. G. Page finished Gilbert's flight. Another pilot brought Gilbert's body home on Christmas Day, and his family laid him to rest a day later. After a year of night flights, 31 of the initial airmail pilots had died. Three years after Gilbert died, commercial aviation took over the airmail service.

CLARENCE AUDBURN GILBERT

WHAT: The first airmail pilot to die

WHERE: Plainville Post Office, 111 S Main, Plainville

COST: Free

PRO TIP: Learn about Lorenzo Fuller, the first Black man to host a television show, at the Rooks County Museum in nearby Stockton.

On June 10, 1967, Congressman Bob Dole dedicated Gilbert's memorial outside the Plainville Post Office. Gilbert's widow had commissioned her husband's bust, which stands on an engraved stone by the building's entrance.

"NO MAIL, LOW MORALE"

What was the 6888th Central Postal Battalion?

Imagine being tired, cold, hungry, and lonely on a battlefield thousands of miles from home. You've received no mail, so you feel like no one cares.

During World War II, the military post office stacked 18 million pieces of mail in unheated, dark, rat-infested Quonset huts in Birmingham, England, while personnel longed for letters. A general predicted that solving this crisis would require six months.

At the same time, Black women pushed to serve their country overseas. The war department took this opportunity to create the 6888th Central Postal Directory Battalion. Major Charity Adams commanded 824 Black enlisted women and 31 officers in the "Six Triple Eight." Except for some nurses, they were the only Black women to serve overseas during the war. Their welcome included a German V-1 rocket striking their dock in Glasgow, Scotland, on Valentine's Day, 1945.

The unit worked 24/7 in three eight-hour shifts to resolve the mess with the motto "No mail, low morale." To track

6888TH CENTRAL POSTAL BATTALION

WHAT: The only Black female battalion to serve overseas during World War II.

WHERE: East side of Grant Ave. south of Smith Lake, near Fort Leavenworth's Grant Ave. entrance. Check the fort's entrance requirements: home.army.mil/leavenworth/index.php/my-fort/all-services/gate-information

COST: Free

PRO TIP: Visit the 6888th exhibit at the Richard Allen Cultural Center, 412 Kiowa St., Leavenworth.

service members, they maintained a card library to distinguish duplicates. For example, "Robert Smith" could be 7,500 people. They examined undeliverable mail for clues. The 6888th processed 65,000 pieces of mail each shift, and the six-month backlog dissolved in three. The 6888th repeated its success in Rouen and Paris, France.

As Black women, the 6888th endured unique challenges. The Red Cross segregated recreation by race and gender. Adams decided the Red Cross was inadequate and boycotted the facilities. Instead, the battalion handled its own recreation.

In February 1946, the army disbanded the unit at Fort Dix, New Jersey. They received no official recognition, except Adams received a promotion to lieutenant colonel. However, on November 30, 2018, Fort Leavenworth unveiled a 6888th monument in the Buffalo Soldier Commemorative Area's Circle of Firsts. Adams Earley's 25-inch bust sits on a pedestal listing 500 of the unit members.

Three 6888th personnel, Sergeant Dolores M. Browne and Privates, First Class Mary J. Barlow and Mary H. Bankston, died in a Rouen traffic accident on July 8, 1945. Browne, Barlow, and Bankston rest with honors in the Normandy American Cemetery at Colleville-sur-Mer.

The 6888th arrives in Europe.
Courtesy of the Department of Defense

SUPER SPREADER

Where did the Spanish flu of 1918 start?

Under the headline "Influenza. Kansas—Haskell," a sentence fragment states that Haskell, Kansas, had reported 18 cases of "severe type" influenza. The warning appeared in the April 5, 1918, *Public Health Reports*. The publication listed detailed statistics for many diseases, but not influenza.

Physicians lacked vaccines and antibiotics to fight the H1N1 virus. Therefore, the Spanish flu swept through the world in 1918. The chaos and destruction of World War I exacerbated the spread.

After the pandemic, researchers investigated the source. A Nobel Laureate for Medicine and others concluded that American troops "brought the disease to France." Over-crowded conditions acted as fuel for infection's fire. Ground zero was likely Camp Funston at Fort Riley, the largest of 16 Army training camps. Two hundred fifty soldiers slept in each of the crowded barracks. The conditions were perfect for spreading the disease.

CAMP FUNSTON

WHAT: The possible Spanish flu pandemic's ground zero

WHERE: E Huebner Rd., Fort Riley

COST: Free

PRO TIP: Check the Army's security requirements before visiting Fort Riley: home.army. mil/riley/index.php/about/ visitor-info

The epidemic likely came to Funston from Haskell County. The local newspaper provides potential contact tracing. The *Santa Fe Monitor*'s February 14, 1918, issue said six Sublette citizens had pneumonia. Before Jean resident Dean Nilson returned to Camp Funston, he and his family visited Sublette. Ernest Elliot saw his brother at Funston. His child was sick when he left. On his return, the

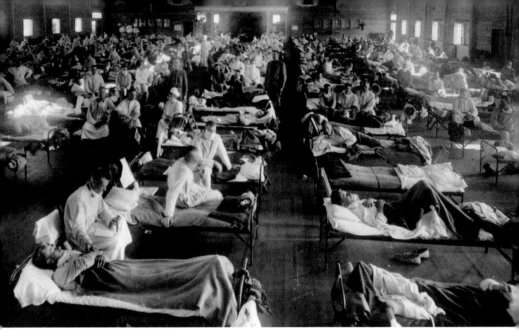

Emergency hospital during influenza epidemic. Courtesy of National Museum of Health and Medicine

child had pneumonia. Dr. Loring Miner reported the illnesses to the US Public Health Service.

Pvt. Albert Getchall, a cook, became Funston's first case on March 4, 1918. By day's end, 107 symptomatic soldiers entered the hospital. On March 9, the Fort Riley *Trench and Camp* reported "a lot of sickness in the form of severe influenza." The disease quickly spread to civilians. By March 17, Lawrence's Haskell Institute had 207 hospitalized flu patients.

The Army shipped infected soldiers overseas, where the disease continued to spread. The illness continued to infect people until the pandemic's end in the early 1920s.

Progress wiped away Camp Funston, but a monument on Huebner Road east of Fort Riley's E Street shows its location. Harry Hardy designed a monument honoring the 10th Sanitary Train soldiers who died of the flu. It stood in Engineers Canyon on Fort Riley's grounds, but the Army tore it down. Its precise location is now lost.

THE ULTIMATE QUACK

Who was the Goat Gland Doctor?

Dr. John Romulus (J. R.) Brinkley became wealthy by restoring his patients' "manly vigor" in his Milford clinic. He rose to fame and fortune by selling quack medicines and filling the airwaves with bad medical advice and good entertainment. But eventually all his influence crashed around him, and he died bankrupt at 57.

Brinkley bought his medical school degree from a diploma mill. The bogus degree allowed him to practice medicine in eight states, including Kansas, and he moved to Milford. When one of his male patients complained that his masculinity was not what it had been, Brinkley seized the opportunity. He inserted a billy goat's parts into the patient. Soon the man's wife conceived, and they named the child Billy—of course.

From then on, Brinkley claimed to cure male flaccidity by inserting goat testicles into his patients' gonads. Many of them claimed that the operation had healed them. The word spread, and Brinkley performed more than 16,000 operations. Brinkley marketed the surgery, extending his impact into mass media, entertainment, and politics.

He bought the radio station KFKB (Kansas First, Kansas Best) in 1923 and installed it in Milford. Brinkley broadcasted patients' letters and prescribed medicines. Five hundred participating druggists sold his prescriptions, which were often

"DOCTOR" J. R. BRINKLEY

WHAT: The quacky Viagra precursor

WHERE: Geary County Historical Society, 530 N Adams St., Junction City

COST: Free

PRO TIP: Milford is now the home of Milford State Park and Milford Reservoir. Fish, camp, and play water sports at the state's largest lake.

Goat Gland Doctor exhibit at the Geary County Historical Society Museum

just colored water. A 1929 *Radio Digest* poll voted KFKB the nation's best station.

However, the *Kansas City Star* owned WDAF, which had lost revenue to KFKB. The American Medical Association also disliked Brinkley. Both groups had Brinkley investigated, and he lost both his radio and medical licenses in 1930 as a result.

Brinkley ran for Kansas governor that year as a write-in and officially placed third. However, Attorney General William Smith tossed any ballot that didn't specify "J. R. Brinkley" despite a 1923 state statute that said officials should honor voter intent. Brinkley had likely won, but he didn't contest the results. Instead, he eventually established a 75,000-watt radio station in Mexico. Lawsuits, the IRS, and mail fraud investigations soon bankrupted him. He died broke in San Antonio on May 26, 1942.

In Arkansas, Johnny Cash first heard the Carter Family—comprising his future wife and in-laws—who performed twice daily on XERA, Brinkley's station.

TAKE YOUR MEDICINE

Do all pharmacists have scruples?

Jack Crispin's Drug Store Museum in Lincoln overflows with vintage pharmacy equipment and supplies. But don't confuse his displays with random clutter. Crispin knows each item's story, and he tells them skillfully.

Crispin began working in a pharmacy at age 16. He then graduated from the University of Kansas and opened a drugstore in Lincoln. In the process, he amassed a plethora of pharmaceutical collectibles, and his wife, Kathie, collected scout memorabilia. The Crispins bought Lincoln's Cummins Block Building to house their collections. His collection inhabits the building's west side, and hers is on the east side.

Crispin's collection focuses on the four decades between 1880 and 1920. During that time, druggists changed from manufacturing medicines to buying prepared products. Crispin will often demonstrate pill preparation techniques.

Some items are terrifying. For example, the Kilacold Chlorine Bomb looks like a teardrop with an elongated tip. "Bomb the first sneeze with Kilacold," its advertising said. Instructions told users to break off the end and let the gas permeate the room, promising that the sufferer's cold would vanish within an hour. Never mind that chlorine gas had killed 1,100 soldiers in World War I's Battle of Ypres. The

Go next door to Kathie Crispin's Post Rock Scout Museum to see memorabilia from Girl Scouts, Boy Scouts, Pioneer Girls, Campfire Girls, and other youth organizations.

company's cringeworthy 1927 advertisement said, "Thousands of doctors declare the late war worthwhile because it gave the world the chlorine treatment."

Horrifying as the chlorine bomb is, Crispin's fleams and asthma treatments are far scarier. Doctors believed for millennia that imbalanced humors caused disease. They extracted blood until the patient passed out. Often, the patient received a new infection instead of healing. Asthma patients could puff on Asthmador Cigarettes to obtain relief. The package said it contained no tobacco. What it did have, stramonium and belladonna, caused hallucinations.

Of course, every object isn't a horror-movie prop. A tiny box of pharmacy measures includes "scruples," one-third of a dram. The special typewriters have keys for scruples, grams, and ounces.

"THE LITTLE NURSE FOR LITTLE ILLS"

How did a Mentholatum dealer help end World War II?

Before the 1906 Food and Drug Act, many medicines were ineffective at best and poisonous at worst. So, when a product actually worked, it had a better chance at success.

Albert Alexander Hyde had lost $100,000 in the 1887 Kansas real estate crash. He desperately sought to support his family. He formed the Yucca Company with two partners, supplying $500 and the factory space.

One health-care product, the Vest Pocket Cough Specific, showed particular promise. Menthol, extracted from Japanese peppermint plants, soothed customers' throats. Hyde turned his kitchen into a lab to make cough syrup with it. In 1894, Hyde produced an ointment with menthol, camphor, and petrolatum, which he named Mentholatum.

Mentholatum quickly topped the company's sales charts. Eight years later, Yucca was renamed for its best product. One of their slogans was "The Little Nurse for Little Ills." The company built factories in Wichita and Buffalo, New York, but when Hyde died in 1935, the company left Wichita.

MENTHOLATUM

WHAT: A patent medicine that worked

WHERE: Wichita-Sedgwick County Historical Museum, 204 S Main St., Wichita

COST: $5 for adults, $2 for children aged 6–12, and free for children under age 6.

PRO TIP: The Spice Merchant, 1300 E Douglas Ave., Wichita, currently inhabits the Mentholatum Building.

William Merrell Vories of Leavenworth brought Mentholatum to Ōmihachiman, Japan. In 1918, his Ōmi Mission founded a tuberculosis hospital and schools known as Vories Gakuen. Two years later, he established Ōmi Sales Company to produce Mentholatum under license. Before World War II began, Vories had obtained Japanese citizenship. However, his Christian faith caused suspicion, and the government shuttered his businesses except for Mentholatum because Japanese soldiers depended on it.

To help end the war, former Japanese Prime Minister Prince Fumimaro Konoe used Vories as a channel to General Douglas MacArthur. He suggested that Emperor Hirohito might renounce his divinity to become a constitutional monarch. MacArthur accepted Hirohito's offer, and the war ended. Vories later met Hirohito four times.

Vories died in 1964. In 1988, Rohto Pharmaceutical bought Mentholatum and now sells it worldwide. Ōmihachiman became Leavenworth's sister city on May 24, 1997.

Hyde supported the Greater Wichita YMCA, the Wichita Children's Home, and the Wesley Hospital and Nurses Training School. The Y's Camp Hyde bears his name.

"THE HEALTHIEST STATE IN THE UNION"

Who stopped people from drinking from the same cup?

> "Kansas is being sterilized . . . from Garden City to Fort Scott and from the Missouri River to the Colorado line." —*Wichita Daily Eagle*, April 23, 1911

While Dr. Samuel J. Crumbine was riding a train, he saw a tuberculosis (TB) patient spitting on the floor and drinking from a common cup. Then a mother poured water from that cup and gave it to her child. Crumbine was horrified. He started campaigning against shared drinking cups. He crusaded against more diseases with slogans like "Swat the Fly" and "Don't Spit on the Sidewalk." Thanks to his vigilance, Kansas banned common cups in 1909 and shared towels two years later.

Under Crumbine's influence, brickmakers stamped "Don't Spit on the Sidewalk" into their paving bricks. One Topeka brickmaker supposedly added the don't-spit slogan on every fourth brick to make Crumbine go away. Boy Scouts helped people install screened windows. Weir City Scoutmaster Frank H. Rose trimmed screen leftovers and attached them to handles, a clever tool that Crumbine called flyswatters.

Crumbine inspired the character Galen "Doc" Adams in the television show *Gunsmoke*. The actor, Milburn Stone, grew up in Burrton. He has a star on the Dodge City Trail of Fame and is in the Boot Hill Museum's Kansas Cowboy Hall of Fame.

Crumbine began his practice in Dodge City. In 1904, he became the Kansas State Board of Health Secretary, and the Crumbines moved to Topeka. By 1911, the *Daily Eagle* said Crumbine was "making Kansas the healthiest state in the Union." Later in 1911, the University of Kansas School of Medicine hired him as its part-time dean.

Crumbine was still in office during the Spanish flu pandemic. He directed the people of Kansas to lock down and mandated masks. Kansans suffered less than those in Colorado or Missouri, but Crumbine's tenure was about to end.

Incoming governor Jonathan M. Davis ordered the health board to fire Crumbine in 1923. They refused, so Davis demanded that Crumbine resign. When Herbert Hoover's American Child Health Association hired him, he moved with his family to New York. Despite Davis's behavior, Crumbine confessed to a "nostalgic longing for the Kansas prairies" in his 1948 autobiography.

DR. SAMUEL J. CRUMBINE

WHAT: The Kansas public health champion

WHERE: Samuel J. Crumbine Pocket Park, 212 SW 8th Ave., Topeka

COST: Free

PRO TIP: Because Crumbine promoted food safety, the National Environmental Health Association annually confers the Samuel J. Crumbine Consumer Protection Award. Recipients are local environmental health jurisdictions that provide outstanding food protection services.

STAND AND DELIVER IN TEACHER TOWN USA

Which city honors the nation's best teachers?

In 1989, Emporia State University, the Emporia school board, and the chamber of commerce decided that their city should host the National Teachers Hall of Fame (NTHF). After all, Emporia State was the first Kansas teacher-training school. The city's dedication to education gives it the nickname Teacher Town USA.

The NTHF inducts five educators every year. After events in Washington, DC, they come to Emporia for Induction Week. The city holds a parade and numerous events. But, the pinnacle is the induction ceremony at the National Teachers Hall of Fame. Afterward, the inductees visit Disney World.

To qualify for the hall of fame, nominees must have worked as certified full-time elementary or secondary teachers for at least 20 years. Nominees must complete a 23-page form and include a résumé and six personal statements, plus five recommendation letters. The essays total 3,000 words. Semifinalists must submit a three-minute video. The selection committee reviews the completed nominations, then it narrows the field to 10 and then to the five inductees.

NATIONAL TEACHERS HALL OF FAME

WHAT: Enshrining America's best educators

WHERE: Visser Hall 114–115, Emporia State University, 1701 Morse Rd., Emporia

COST: Free

PRO TIP: Honor more than 400 Kansas teachers at the Kansas Teachers Hall of Fame in Dodge City.

Dennis Rogers, a member of the Navajo tribe, plays a Native American flute during the Kansas Day Business Expo on Saturday, January 25, 2020, at Paola Middle School. Courtesy of the Miami County Republic.

Kansas Day observances spread west to Bird City. In 1888, Kansas Day fell on Sunday, so the school celebrated the holiday on Monday. Six students spoke and Walter Colt gave his "Kansas as a Temperance State" address.

Paola celebrated Kansas Day each year until the pandemic killed the celebration. Bird City celebrated the occasion for some time but stopped. Then in 1930, the city resumed the custom. The Mother's Circle of the Bird City Methodist Church organized a Kansas Day Picnic, which lasted all day. Bird City has celebrated Kansas Day ever since. While Paola and Bird City have celebrated the most, many other locales annually say, "Happy Birthday, Kansas!"

The Republican Party formed men's and women's Kansas Day Clubs. They met annually in Topeka. The Democratic Party decided to celebrate statehood on February 22 because Abraham Lincoln had raised the first 34-star flag in Philadelphia on February 22, 1861.

THE BISON'S SAVIOR

How did a buffalo hunter become the species' savior?

In the 1870s, the fact that bison had been hunted almost to extinction forced Native Americans to surrender and accept life on the reservation. Up until then, Plains indigenous cultures had relied on bison for food, furniture, tools, and sacred objects.

As a hunter, C. J. "Buffalo" Jones had regularly slaughtered up to 60 bison daily. He came to Western Kansas to hunt but became one of Garden City's founders. He induced two railroads to stop in the new city, and the citizens elected him the city's first mayor.

Somewhere along the way, Jones reversed course and became the bison's savior. In Kansas, numerous ranchers had replaced the bison with cattle. Then the 1880s' brutal winters produced chest-high snow, and many cattle died. Since bison could withstand harsher weather than cattle, in 1886, Jones decided to breed bison with cattle to build a hardier herd of "cattalo." To accomplish this, he had to search all the way from the Texas Panhandle to Canada to find some bison. In Manitoba, he outbid the government for 86 of the endangered animals. He eventually collected 140 of them.

Jones and other interested ranchers were just in time. While they searched for bison, the Smithsonian was also

C. J. "BUFFALO" JONES

WHAT: From bison hunter to bison savior

WHERE: Finney County Historical Museum, 403 S 4th St., Garden City

COST: Donation

PRO TIP: Visit the Lee Richardson Zoo's bison exhibit after visiting the museum's Jones exhibit. The museum stands adjacent to the zoo entrance.

Buffalo Jones exhibit

looking. Chief Taxidermist William Temple Hornady killed and preserved 44 Montana bison for some of the US National Museum dioramas. Hornady's trophies almost wiped out Montana's bison herd. (He later saved six live bison as the National Zoo's director.)

The cattalo experiment failed, but Jones had made powerful friends who were interested in bison preservation. President Theodore Roosevelt appointed him as Yellowstone National Park's first game warden. Jones brought three bulls to Yellowstone to increase the number of native bison. When he arrived, only 23 Yellowstone bison remained. The following year, the park superintendent reported that the herd was flourishing.

After Jones left Yellowstone, he took the author Zane Grey to lasso mountain lions in Arizona. Grey became a Western writer and modeled his heroes after Jones. He also wrote Jones's biography, *The Last of the Plainsmen*.

Jones's statue stands on the Finney County Courthouse grounds. He built the county's original courthouse.

THE FOREST THAT DIDN'T TAKE

What happened to the Kansas National Forest?

"People do not master their environment.
They bargain with it." —Historian Elliott West

The Arkansas River Valley between Garden City and the Colorado line is more conducive to growing sagebrush and grasses than trees. However, in 1906, the government tried to turn the river's south side into a 302,387-acre wood. Unfortunately, the project failed.

So why plant a forest where none ever existed? The story starts in the Nebraska Sandhills. At the urging of University of Nebraska botany Professor Charles E. Bessey, Professor Lawrence Bruner hand-planted 13,000 trees on his Sandhills ranch. Ten years later, his trees stood 18 feet tall. The success inspired President Theodore Roosevelt to establish three national forests in Nebraska and the Bessey Nursery. The nursery's seedlings still supply conservation districts and national forests throughout the region.

Federal foresters were concerned about the arid climate in the Southwest Kansas sand hills. Why not try to duplicate the successful Nebraska experiment in Kansas? Planting began in 1906 with Bessey Nursery seedlings. Yellow pines and honey locusts did best, but more than two-thirds of

KANSAS NATIONAL FOREST

WHAT: How the weather killed the Kansas National Forest

WHERE: Sandsage Bison Range Wildlife Area

COST: $20

PRO TIP: Sandsage has a forest remnant in the corner of a pasture. Check the Friends of Sandsage Bison Range's website for tour information.

those trees died. All the other species also died. In March 1907, a prairie fire destroyed the remainder.

The US Forest Service refused to quit despite the seeming futility of the project. Instead, they planted about 125,000 seedlings annually for several more years. Administrators Carlos Bates and Roy Pierce reported that an "extreme drought" had killed almost the entire planting four years after the fire. In response, the forest service tried Nebraska-proven Jack pine. Unfortunately, that, too, failed. Even the notoriously hardy red cedar died. Bates and Pierce blamed "the greater warmth . . ., the more extreme drought, and the greater severity of the summer winds."

Futility won. In 1923 the *Topeka Capital* wrote the forest's obituary. "All of the former Kansas National Forest is now grown up to soapweed, cactus, and clear, invigorating prairie air."

President Woodrow Wilson abolished the forest project in 1915, except for several sections the state received for a big-game preserve. The preserve is now the Sandsage Bison Range, where the once-endangered buffalo continue to roam.

WHEN THE BRIDE CAME HOME TO COTTONWOOD RANCH

Why did Jennie Pratt cry when she saw her new home?

Abraham Pratt filed a Homestead Act claim in 1878 on the site of present-day Studley. His son Fent joined his father in March 1880. Two years later, Tom Pratt, Abraham's younger son, joined them. They lived in a dugout, a hole in the ground with a roof.

Jennie (Place) Pratt had arrived in Lenora from Yorkshire, England, on December 30, 1888. She married John Fenton "Fent" Pratt the next day. He took her home on New Year's Day. When she saw the one-room stone house her husband had built for her, Jennie burst into tears. Imagine her response if Fent had brought her to a dugout.

Even if Fent had explained pioneer life, Jennie was unprepared for the treeless land. She tried to escape by walking 21 miles to the railroad depot in Lenora while her husband was tending sheep. Each time she tried to leave, the neighbors detained her until Fent came to bring her back. By the time baby Hilda arrived on October 2, 1889,

COTTONWOOD RANCH STATE HISTORIC SITE

WHAT: Pioneer's sheep ranch

WHERE: 14432 E Hwy. 24, Studley

COST: Donation

PRO TIP: The ranch buildings are open on Thursdays through Saturdays from May 1 to September 30. Otherwise, enjoy a self-guided tour during daylight.

Jennie had accepted her life. The Pratts welcomed baby Elsie on September 23, 1894.

Tom married Elizabeth Mosier in 1897, and they had six children.

Fent became an avid photographer. His meticulous records show that the house had two wings and outbuildings in a U shape behind it in the 1890s. Since homesteaders could gain extra land by planting trees, Fent ordered hundreds of them, and some still grow today. The cottonwoods around the house gave Cottonwood Ranch its name.

Jennie eventually adapted. She sheared sheep and planted flowers and herbs while Fent grew vegetables and trees. Fent died in 1937 and Jennie continued to live at the ranch until her death in 1959. Elsie married Clarence Johnson and moved to Manhattan, but Hilda remained until 1978. She died in 1980. The state bought the ranch three years later, and it became a state historic site. The house retains the Pratts' furnishings, and most outbuildings remain.

Studley is the only town in Kansas without a city limits sign. The Kansas Department of Transportation quit installing the signs because people stole them as fast as KDOT could replace them. Look for the Studley sign in a hall at Cottonwood Ranch.

PUTTING WHEAT IN THE WHEAT STATE

How did Kansas become the Wheat State?

"Much of the credit for making Kansas a great wheat state belongs to one man, the late Bernhard Warkentin of Newton."—F. D. Coburn, Kansas State Board of Agriculture Secretary

Russian Empress Catherine the Great enticed Prussian Mennonites to move to Russian-dominated Ukraine. She gave them land, religious freedom, and immunity from military service for 100 years. Bernhard Warkentin Sr. had developed Turkey Red Wheat in the Molotschna (Milk River) Colony. Because the exemption was ending, the Germans from Russia were anxious to leave. Several families emigrated to Kansas and brought their Turkey Red Wheat seeds with them.

In 1872 and 1873, Warkentin Jr. and others explored the United States, looking for a favorable location. After searching over 10,000 miles, the group chose Kansas. The first Mennonites settled in Halstead, Newton, and Moundridge. Warkentin established a mill in Halstead. Later that year, the Mennonite Board of Guardians appointed Warkentin as their agent. He influenced 12,000 Mennonites to choose Kansas. In 1875, Warkentin married Wilhelmina Eisenmayer in Summerfield, Illinois. The Warkentins remained in Halstead until 1885. After touring Europe, they moved to Newton.

Before the Mennonites brought Turkey Red, Kansans didn't grow much wheat. Legend credits Anna Barkman, an eight-year-old girl who picked two gallons of Turkey Red kernels in the Ukraine and transported them to the US. The Barkmans reputedly harvested their wheat in Kansas in 1875.

Sherman County wheat

In reality, every family coming from Russia had brought seed wheat with them.

Turkey Red did not become the standard wheat for some time. Mills could not grind the hard wheat, and obtaining sufficient seed was difficult. Warkentin installed equipment that could mill the hard grain. In 1900, he arranged to import about 15,000 bushels of seed wheat.

In 1908, the Warkentins visited the Middle East. While traveling from Damascus to Beirut, someone accidentally fired a pistol in the next train compartment, mortally wounding Mr. Warkentin.

Beyond Warkentin's numerous business interests, he helped found Bethel College, the Bethel Deaconess Hospital, and the Mennonite Mutual Fire Insurance Company.

CREEPY CRAWLIES

Would you pet a tarantula?

"It's an opportunity to face your fears."—Taellor Howland, K-State Insect Zoo docent

The Addams family was creepy, kooky, mysterious, and spooky, but they have nothing on the K-State Insect Zoo. K-State could name the insectarium "the Arthropod Zoo" because the collection includes more than insects. Millipedes, centipedes, spiders, and crustaceans all inhabit the museum's collections.

The former K-State dairy barn houses the zoo. The barn's exterior explains what you're in for: three-dimensional giant insects attached to the wall crawl from the door toward the roof's peak. Inside, a wall of preserved insects attracts visiting humans, showcasing only a small portion of the world's one million insect species.

The tarantulas and scorpions induce skin-crawling reactions, but the real horrors await in the mock kitchen. Open the drawers and view the dastardly denizens lurking in your kitchen's dark corners. Turn on the black light in the scorpions' terrarium and watch them reflect the ultraviolet. The light paints them a shade of teal.

Book a tour and the docents will let you pet a tarantula and other creepy crawlies. Docent Taellor Howland said "The first

THE INSECT ZOO

WHAT: Manhattan insectarium

WHERE: 1500 Denison Ave., Kansas State University, Manhattan

COST: $3 for everyone age three and up. The Insect Zoo offers self-guided tours on afternoons from Tuesday through Saturday. Schedule a private guided tour at insect-zoo.appointlet.com. Prices start at $28.

PRO TIP: Follow the parking instructions at k-state.edu/butterfly/directions.html.

reaction is, 'I don't want to touch it.'" However, guests soon want to learn more. Docents caution that before you stomp on a spider, remember that they hunt other insects and keep bug populations in check.

Watch the diligent leafcutter ants as they trim leaves and feed fungus, which provides food for the ants. The keepers drop the leaves into an open dish. Teflon covers the dish's interior so the ants can't escape.

Insect zoo

A transparent beehive shows bees constructing their honeycombs and filling them with honey. Bees need flower nectar to produce honey. As they gather nectar, they pollinate the plants. Bees are crucial to agriculture because they pollinate up to 85 percent of food crops.

K-State's horticulture students develop and maintain the K-State Garden surrounding the Insect Zoo. Pick up self-guided tour instructions in the wooden birdhouse beside the welcome sign. Please recycle the guide by returning it to the wooden guide holder. In November, the garden sells poinsettias and amaryllis plants.

THE OCTAGONAL VEGETARIANS

Where was the vegetarian utopia?

"We have all come [to Octagon City], have brought our mothers, our fathers, and our little ones, and find no shelter sufficient to shield them."—Miriam Colt, Octagon City resident

Frontiers are magnets for often-strange social experiments, and Octagon City was stranger than most. Prospective citizens had to swear that they would become vegetarians and avoid tea, coffee, and other stimulants. And they had to consent to live in octagonal buildings in octagon-shaped communities.

Dr. John McLaurin, an Octagon City founder, inspected the townsite in May 1856. He laid out eight squares for Octagon Villages, but promoters did little to prepare the site for settlement. They had charged the settlers $10 apiece to construct a mill but didn't build one.

Miriam Colt and her family arrived on May 12, 1858. "Not a house is to be seen," she wrote. "All is not right." The organizers had promised to build mills and a temporary boarding house but they never materialized. Instead, everyone was forced to camp out. No infrastructure was present, and the site was miles from

OCTAGON CITY

WHAT: A failed frontier utopia

WHERE: A marker stands at Arizona Rd. and 150th St. A bridge crosses Vegetarian Creek one mile west of Highway 169 and Arizona Road six miles southeast of Humboldt.

COST: Free

PRO TIP: The settlers' campsite location is uncertain.

Vegetarian Creek

other settlements. The families feared attacks from both Border Ruffians and Native American warriors.

The settlers contracted malaria from mosquitoes and dysentery from bad water. Many pioneers fled the community, but the Colts were too ill. Finally, in September, they escaped, but the Colts' troubles were far from over. Within nine days of leaving Octagon City, Miriam's son and husband died from dysentery. Before the year ended, both her father- and mother-in-law had died in Octagon City.

By the following spring, all the settlers had deserted Octagon City. The Stewart family stayed in Kansas but moved northwest to Cottage Grove.

The Octagonians were supposed to avoid coffee. Yet, ironically, a Humboldt coffee shop, Octagon City Coffee Co., bears their settlement's name.

DON'T COMPETE WITH THE JAMES GANG

Why did the Daltons want to rob two banks at once?

"We're going to beat anything Jesse James ever did—rob two banks at once, in broad daylight."

—Bob Dalton

The Dalton Gang rode into Coffeyville on October 5, 1892. They intended to do something no one had accomplished, rob two banks simultaneously in daylight. The James-Younger Gang members were their cousins, whom they longed to outdo.

They failed. By the end of the incident, four gang members and four citizens had died.

The robbers had intended to hitch their horses on Eighth Street to ease their respective escapes. However, Eighth Street was under construction so they stashed their horses in an alley instead.

The Daltons had lived in Coffeyville, so they were well known enough for Aleck McKenna to recognize one of them. When the gang split and ran into the banks, McKenna saw a robber point a gun at a C. M. Condon & Co. Bank employee. He shouted, "The bank is being robbed!" The word spread and H. H. Isham distributed his store's firearms.

THE DALTON DEFENDERS

WHAT: The robbers who overreached

WHERE: Dalton Defenders and Coffeyville History Museum, 814 S Walnut St., Coffeyville

COST: $8 for adults, $7 for seniors and veterans, $6 children 6–17, under 6 free with adult admission.

PRO TIP: The Condon Bank is now the Coffeyville Chamber of Commerce. Tour the Daltons' target.

Inside the bank, Condon cashier C. M. Ball pretended that the safe stayed locked for three more minutes. Grat Dalton said he'd wait. The delay was fatal. Bullets crashed through Condon's windows, and the robbers fled.

Bob and Emmett Dalton entered First National Bank—cashier Thomas Ayres also tried to stall but eventually the gang obtained $20,000. They heard shots and left. Bob shot Lucius M. Baldwin, Charles Brown, and George Cubine, his childhood friend, in the alley. Emmett shot Ayres.

Isham and L. A. Dietz crouched behind two cookstoves while a dozen men barricaded the alley with a wagon. Because of the citizens' quick response, the robbers faced a 300-foot gauntlet of gunfire. After three minutes, all the bandits were on the ground. Only Emmett had survived. Marshal Charles T. Connally had died between two bandits.

A court sentenced Emmett to 25 years for his crimes. He served 14 before Governor Edward Hoch pardoned him in 1907. He became a movie star in California.

Eva (Dalton) Whipple lived in Meade. The Whipples left Meade after her brothers perished in Coffeyville. Legend says that cowboys mysteriously appeared inside the Whipples' former home. The new owners investigated and discovered a tunnel. It's now the Dalton Gang Hideout Museum, 502 S Pearlette St., Meade 67864.

THE FATAL FINGERPRINT

Why was a murder near Elkader a forensic science milestone?

At 1:10 p.m. on May 23, 1927, the Fleagle Gang burst into the First National Bank of Lamar, Colorado, intending to rob it. Bank president A. N. "Newt" Parrish shot Howard "Heavy" Royston in the jaw and the men continued to exchange fire. Parrish missed, but Royston didn't. Jake Fleagle murdered J. F. "Jaddo" Parrish, Newt's son, with a shot in the back.

The robbers absconded with nearly $250,000 worth of loot, and two hostages, Edward Lundgren and Everett Kesinger. They raced out of Lamar in a blue Buick. Sheriff Lloyd E. Alderman chased them, then Ralph Fleagle stopped the car and ejected Lundgren. Ralph used Kesinger as a human shield and shot up Alderman's Studebaker. Then they drove into Kansas, unpursued.

The gang stopped at the Fleagles' ranch near Marienthal. Royston needed a doctor, so they induced Dr. William Wineinger of Dighton to help them. After he patched up Royston, the bandits murdered the doctor in a canyon south of Elkader. They pushed his car and his body off a cliff. They then murdered Kesinger in an abandoned shack near Liberal and scattered.

They might have gotten away with it but Jake had left one fingerprint on Wineinger's car window. Al Ground, a federal fingerprint specialist, memorized it. When police arrested William Harrison Holden in California, Ground matched his fingerprints to Jake, who had served time in Oklahoma. The match proved that Holden was an alias. Then Ground remembered the print from the Lamar bank robbery. The files verified Ground's memory. The Bureau of Investigation, now the FBI, had their man.

The post office tracked Ralph to Kankakee, Illinois. Alderman located Royston in California and George Abshier

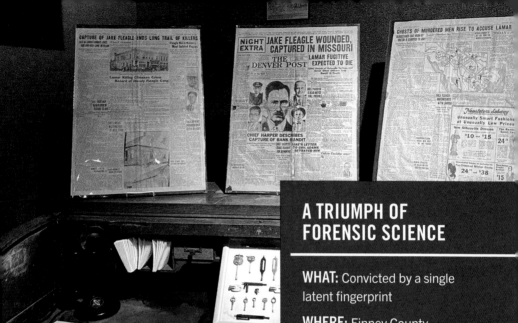

Fleagle coverage

A TRIUMPH OF FORENSIC SCIENCE

WHAT: Convicted by a single latent fingerprint

WHERE: Finney County Historical Society Museum, 403 S 4th St., Garden City

COST: Donation

PRO TIP: Wineinger's car window is the centerpiece of the museum's notorious crimes exhibit. The Lane County Museum in Dighton has case records.

in Grand Junction, Colorado. Colorado executed them in July 1930. The postal inspectors tracked Jake to Branson, Missouri, three months later. He pulled a gun, and the officers shot him. He died a few hours later.

The Fleagle case was the first time the bureau had connected a criminal to a crime with a single latent fingerprint.

Kansas attracted other criminal activity. In April 2018, a tunnel collapsed at the former Bundy Hotel in Hugoton, now a Farm Bureau agency. The collapse revealed numerous bottles from Dr. Elwood Bundy's practice. Legend says Bonnie Parker and Clyde Barrow ran a bootlegging operation in Hugoton, and he gambled at the hotel.

THE VANISHING SERIAL KILLERS

What happened to the Bloody Benders?

People disappeared on the frontier—whether voluntarily or involuntarily. The Homestead Act enabled people to leave their old lives behind and escape civilization. Some of them ran into people like the Bender crime family. Ma and Pa Bender spoke in thick German accents. The younger Benders, Kate and John, sounded more American. They built a cabin near Cherryvale and offered to feed and house travelers along the Osage Mission Trail. The community blamed horse thieves for three victims found with crushed skulls and evidence of stolen horses near the cabin.

Then the Benders killed the wrong man. When Dr. William York went missing in 1873, his brother Ed, a colonel in Fort Scott, went looking. He dismissed the Benders as "dim-witted country folks," but they were bright enough to flee.

A month later, the Benders' neighbor Billy Tole noticed their starving animals and a bad smell coming from the Benders' cabin. He and Civil War veteran Leroy Dick went to investigate. Dick recognized the overpowering stench of dead bodies. Investigators discovered a blood-soaked cellar and multiple corpses on the property, including Dr. York's. Kate had probably distracted guests while the other Benders smashed in their

The Benders, a.k.a. the "Bloody Benders"

victims' skulls and robbed them. They probably killed more than 20 people.

A ticket agent in Thayer claimed he had sold tickets to four people who matched the Benders' descriptions. Then the trail disappeared. Governor Thomas Osborn and Senator Alexander York offered rewards, but no one claimed them. The military was too busy fighting to help. The "Bloody Benders'" crimes hit the nation's front pages, and Bender sightings piled up in Missouri, Texas, Oklahoma, New Mexico, Colorado, and California.

In 1880, a man claiming to be Pa Bender appeared in Colfax County, Nebraska, but he was a hoaxer. The *Cherryvale Globe* said, "The people of Labette and Montgomery counties believe that the Benders escaped . . . Any statement to the contrary is false."

In 2013, *True West* magazine presented a case that Colorado café owners John and Katie Bender were John and Kate Bender of Bloody Bender infamy.

ARTIST PROVOCATEUR

What inspired M. T. Liggett?

"Working on my art, I was always in a fury of one kind or another. But doing it worked out all the ornery."
—M. T. Liggett

Mullinville doesn't need city limits or welcome signs. Myron Thomas (M. T.) Liggett ensured that no one would miss his hometown. On the west, a quarter-mile stream of waving whirligigs and tall totems demands attention on Highway 400. A similar strip on the eastern end compels Highway 54 drivers to take notice.

Liggett was an equal-opportunity provocateur. By default, he took the opposite position from any questioners. When he disagreed with something, his art let the world know. If a citizen upset him, a sculpture appeared in a strategic location. One of his totems announced, "Mullinville Self-Anointed Elitist Bourgeois."

"If you walk up to me and say you're a Democrat, I'm a Republican. If you're a Buddhist, I'm a Shinto. If you're a Catholic, I'm a Protestant," he said. Whatever his opinions,

M. T. LIGGETT ART ENVIRONMENT

WHAT: Mullinville's star artist

WHERE: 207 Elm St., Mullinville

COST: Donation

PRO TIP: While in Kiowa County, visit Greensburg's Big Well Museum 11 miles east of Mullinville.

Stop by the visitor center first for an introduction. Then examine Liggett's creations along Mullinville's highways.

he was prolific. He filled his 70 acres with approximately 600 metal works. When he died in 2017, the *New York Times* and the *Washington Post* ran his obituary.

A seven- or eight-year-old kid is the best artist, he believed. He was that kid. A teacher told him to draw a cow. He only had a purple crayon, so he drew a purple cow. The teacher ridiculed him, and he dropped art for decades. Liggett resented censorship after that.

The Kohler Foundation conserved Liggett's works after his 2017 death. Five years later, the foundation transferred the art and visitor center's ownership to Greensburg's 5.4.7 Art Center. A purple cow and a pair of calves stand proudly behind glass in the center.

To find the studio, look for the big yellow arrow labeled "Stew-Dee-Owe." The center exhibits Liggett's custom tools and other artifacts from his studio.

FINE ART FROM FOUND OBJECTS

How did Lester Raymer's early life influence his art?

> "When I'm working in a medium, the medium itself brings on the ideas. I never understood why an artist couldn't work in more than one medium."
>
> —Lester Raymer

Lester Wilton Raymer grew up on a farm outside Alva, Oklahoma, where his mother conducted daily Bible readings. Blacksmith skills were essential for a farm boy, but Raymer's relentless creativity extended into multiple media and he eventually made his way to art school in Chicago. Alva was on the circus circuit and, to pay for his schooling, Raymer worked for a poultry factory. He eventually incorporated all these influences into his art.

At the Chicago Art Institute (CAI), Raymer met his future wife, Ramona Weddle, who became an art instructor at Bethany College in Lindsborg. Raymer majored in painting and printmaking at CAI, but other media lured his attention as well. After he graduated in 1933, he established an art studio at the family farm in Alva until 1945.

Lester and Ramona married in 1945. He taught art at Bethany for a year, and then the couple established the Red Barn Studio. Raymer incorporated biblical themes, horses, roosters, and circus motifs into his artwork.

RED BARN STUDIO

WHAT: An artist in many media

WHERE: 212 S Main St., Lindsborg

COST: Donation

PRO TIP: The Red Barn has an active artists-in-residence program.

Raymer admired Spanish old masters, and they also prominently influenced his work.

The Raymers built their studio and home with recycled materials. He enjoyed turning found objects into fine art. He gathered items from the dump, garage sales, auctions, and salvage yards. He brought home whatever looked interesting. While

Lester Raymer's toys and painting

Raymer was creating artwork for sale, he did not neglect his family. Each year, he created a Christmas gift for Ramona. From 1960 on, the gifts were always toys.

In 1997, five years after the Raymers' deaths, the Raymer Society for the Arts opened the Red Barn Studio for tours. Raymer's range is astounding. Look for textiles, wood carvings, metalwork, paintings, and more. The knowledgeable docents point out the found objects that Raymer incorporated because they are often unrecognizable until the docent highlights them.

Bethany College produced other famous artists. Birger Sandzén taught at Bethany for 52 years. In his spare time, Sandzén painted and made prints. Art galleries across the nation exhibited his work. Bethany opened the Sandzén Gallery on campus after his death.

WALK WITH THE DINOSAURS

Who created the Erie dinosaurs?

Jurassic Park meets *Forged in Fire* within a small enclosure in Erie. One story speculates that Robert Dorris created the fantastic beasts for his daughter who loved dinosaurs. Another story says that a 1980s Smithsonian trip inspired him. Perhaps the inspiration was a combination of the two. But first, Dorris had to survive World War II.

He joined the navy during World War II when he was 17 and served on the USS *Princeton*. The ship fought in the battles of Saipan and the Philippine Sea. A dive-bomber struck her during the Battle of Leyte Gulf, and she sank. Dorris was rescued, and then served on the USS *Siboney*. After the war, he worked for General Dynamics in aviation. Eventually, the Dorrises retired to Erie, his wife Elveta's hometown.

Whatever his inspiration, Dorris began creating his *Jurassic Park* fossils in 1989. He photographed dinosaur skeletons and searched junkyards to flesh out his planned creations. Then he forged them in a fire. His designs ranged from a few inches to 30 feet long.

After the Dorrises died, their family donated many of his sculptures to the City of Erie. They hoped the display would attract tourists to the Southeast Kansas city. The fantastic beasts now occupy half a block surrounded by a metal fence. The family endeavored to create a tourist attraction for their hometown but they specified that there must never

Erie hosts the oldest annual military get-together—the Old Soldiers and Sailors Reunion—each July.

ERIE DINOSAUR PARK

WHAT: Dorris's dynamic dinosaurs

WHERE: 4th St. and S Walnut St., Erie

COST: Free

PRO TIP: The gates are officially open on the second Saturday and third Sunday of each month, but guests are welcome to look over the fence during daylight hours.

be a charge for visiting the dinosaurs. Erie has honored their wishes and reinstalled the beasts on concrete pads. Then crews constructed sidewalks and interpretive signs within the steel fence, where visitors can wander to their hearts' content.

Discerning viewers should try to decode the dinosaurs' structure. Which wings are car hoods? Which heads are transmission casings, and which are oil pans? The breadth of Dorris's imagination is astounding. Perhaps they will inspire the next generation of fantastic beasts.

ART OF THE FOSSILS

Where did Vi Fick find all those fossils?

In another eon, what is now Kansas was under the Western Interior Seaway, sometimes called Hell's Aquarium. Apex predators like the mosasaur and the *Xiphactinus audax* patrolled the seaway. Eventually, the sea dried up and stranded these strange creatures on land. But the Kansas chalk is kind to delicate stone bones. Fossil hunters can easily extract intact fossils from the soft chalk.

Ernie and Vi Fick's ranch was a fossil hunter's paradise. In 1964, the couple began collecting fossils. Vi saw the fossils differently than most folks. She saw them as art supplies. When their rock, fossil, and art collection outgrew their home, they donated it to the Fick Fossil and History Museum.

The Ficks' collections are the foundation of the museum's impressive rock and mineral collection. But Vi's grassroots art paintings are the museum's most original pieces. These paintings introduce her unique vision. Her oil painting *Deer at the Lake* turns fossil vertebrae into tree trunks. Oyster shells became leaves, shark teeth emerged as rocks, and fish ribs evolved into branches. The *Deer with a Tree* measures about 18 inches by 15 inches, including the frame. Each "leaf" is a small shark's tooth. Vi displayed her dexterity and patience while carefully attaching each half-inch tooth to the painted background. She melted crayons to color the dinosaur remains and help them stick together. Look for her flag spangled with shark teeth.

FICK FOSSIL AND HISTORY MUSEUM

WHAT: Vi Fick's unusual vision

WHERE: 700 W 3rd St., Oakley

COST: Donation

PRO TIP: Look for the rare mosasaur skull with an intact eye socket.

The museum further explores Logan County's past from prehistory to the 20th century, including a facsimile of a sod house built inside. A museum addition encloses a 1956 Oakley fire engine.

Over the years, Oakley funeral director Don Hall amassed a massive pencil and pen collection from all over the United States. Many are from Kansas, and several came from Oakley.

MONSTER MASH

How did people from Virginia come to start a store in Cawker City?

Matt Alford felt stir-crazy. The COVID-19 pandemic lockdown was unbearable, and he had to get out of town. So he drove from Virginia to the West Coast.

On his way home, he visited Cawker City, home of the world's largest ball of sisal twine. He spotted an old building for sale less than a block from the twine ball. Alford bought it on the spot, and invited his girlfriend, Julie Agee, to join him, which she did. They brought their wonderfully quirky sense of humor with them. They established Eyegore's Curiosities and Monster Museum. The couple later married at the home of the world's largest sisal twine ball.

Matt, Julie, and Goblin the Wonder Cat's emporium feels more like a museum for the demented than a store. A vintage human anatomical torso model; a mummified juvenile Sasquatch; Count Cluckula, the World's Only Vampire Chicken; and Frankenstein's head are all on display. A cast of Sasquatch's big foot hangs on the wall beside his head. While you browse, look for the Pyramid Shriner wildebeest and the contorted werewolf hand from 1558.

You'll never look at a rear-view window the same way after seeing Eyegore's "the Rear View" wall. All kinds of animals moon guests from the wall. An enamel bedpan completes the

CAWKER CITY'S ODDITIES

WHAT: Eyegore's Curiosities and Monster Museum

WHERE: 732 Wisconsin St., Cawker City

COST: Free

PRO TIP: Stay at the Old Station Inn across the street from the ball of twine. It's a vintage gas station complete with gas pumps.

Dorothy and the Winged Monkey

collection. A raccoon dressed as Dorothy Gale, complete with a wig, gingham dress, and wicker basket, sits on a display case. She must have left Toto back in Oz and brought the winged monkey crossed with a squirrel that is strategically placed in the store.

The Monkey's Paw comes with instructions. If you buy it, you get five wishes to "totally be responsible for the fate, existence, and outcome of life as we know it." Are you ready for the burden? You can also buy Ball of Twine souvenirs, unusual pop varieties, and nostalgic candies.

When you feel stir-crazy, you can always escape to Cawker City. The monsters are waiting.

If you're itching to get hitched, Matt will do the honors. Make sure to invite Linda Clover, the Ball of Twine's caretaker. After the ceremony, she'll help you tie the knot with some official sisal twine.

ALONE IN A CAGE

Where is the *Wichita Troll*?

> "[Uncle Tim] can spare a share for a poor old troll, for he don't need his shinbone." —Sam Gamgee, *The Fellowship of the Ring*

If Sam Gamgee is right, people walking along the Arkansas River's east bank in Wichita had better watch out.

A judge has sentenced the *Wichita Troll* to eternal imprisonment for stealing Uncle Tim's shinbone. The jailers have caged the troll in a hole below the ground. A metal grate above his head restrains the troll from escaping. The creature is left open to the elements. Sometimes he nearly drowns.

So where did you come from, *Wichita Troll*? Trolls have mysterious origins, but we have discovered who created Uncle Tim's assaulter. Sculptor Connie Ernatt made the seven-foot-tall troll to add interest to an overflow pit beside the Arkansas River Trail.

Ernatt engraved his face into a perpetual scowl, and chains ensnare his body. He reaches toward the grate, hoping to catch passersby. He successfully hid for three months after his sentence. Fortunately, no one lost a shin. She originally planned for the troll to push a stick through the grate to attract people's attention. That idea didn't work, so the troll only reaches toward the grate.

THE TROLL AWAITS

WHAT: The *Wichita Troll*

WHERE: East of *Keeper of the Plains*, W Central Ave., Wichita

COST: Free

PRO TIP: After attending the Ring of Fire ceremony, staged nightly at the *Keeper of the Plains* statue in downtown Wichita, visit the river's east side, where you can see the troll who glows green at night.

Wichita Troll

She wanted to create a believable creature. "I tried hard not to make [the troll] too cute or too scary, but right in between," she said.

Unfortunately, some of the troll's visitors are abusive. In 2012, someone sawed off the troll's arm and stole his necklace. "They went down there with the intention to do it," Ernatt said. She installed a reinforced arm and replaced the necklace in 2014. Wichita city workers sealed vandals' entry points.

Will we pinpoint the troll's precise location? No, because that would defeat the purpose.

Ernatt and her team, Brady Hatter, John Ernatt, and Karen Cox, created another troll for visitors to Botanica, the Wichita Gardens. This one was allegedly lulled to sleep under Sleeping Troll Hill.

DREAM HORIZON

Where is the world's largest mural painted by a single artist?

A Wichita mural, *El Sueño Original* (*The Original Dream*), is entered in the *Guinness World Records* for being the World's Largest Acrylic Mural Painted by a Single Artist. *El Sueño* swathes the Beachner Grain elevator with depictions of citizens of the neighborhoods that the elevator separates.

Columbian street artist GLeo painted it during the fall of 2014. It spans about 50,000 square feet, which is 12,000 square feet larger than the nearest competitor. How big is it? About the size of a football field standing on its side. The east-facing mural witnesses the sunrise each morning.

The sponsoring Horizontes Project did not intend to set a world record, Director Armando Minjárez said. They discovered it was record-breaking after they had determined the design.

Railroads and giant grain elevators divide two Wichita neighborhoods, providing an industrial corridor that creates a physical, "visual barrier between the

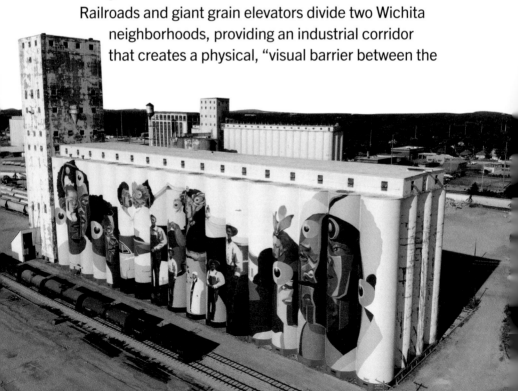

Northeast and the North End." The North End neighborhood is predominantly Latinx. Mostly Black residents have clustered in the Northeast.

One day, Minjárez saw two girls playing with the grain elevators in the distance.

"And I started questioning, 'What if?'" he said. "What if they could decide how their neighborhood was built? What if there was something on that grain elevator? What would their horizon look like?" Minjárez searched for an artist of color and discovered GLeo. The artist and the director worked together on the design. The inspirational girls will see people like them reflected majestically, he said. "That's going to have a positive impact in who they are and who they might become."

A woman in the mural's center wears a skirt represented by a Kitikiti'sh (Wichita) tribe's hut. The tribe built those huts beside the Arkansas River. The woman personifies this diverse city that grew beside the Arkansas River and the people of color who inhabit her land.

EL SUEÑO ORIGINAL (*THE ORIGINAL DREAM*)

WHAT: World's record mural on a grain elevator

WHERE: 519 E 20th St. N, Wichita

COST: Free

PRO TIP: The mural's orange fish eyes represent the elements. Five clustered in a triangle represent the universe.

El Sueño is the most ambitious of the Horizontes Project's murals. Every person depicted in the mural lived in one of the surrounding neighborhoods at one time. The group also sponsored 20 more murals on Wichita's north side.

HOW TO PAINT THE TOWN

How did Clay Center become the Mural Capital of Kansas?

The Clay Center Rotary Club elected Brett Hubka president in 2020. "Every president does a project," he said, "and I tried to figure out what to do." A few years earlier, a Kansas State University student team had proposed a downtown Clay Center plan. It included one downtown mural. Hubka suggested that Rotary sponsor a mural.

Club member Kyle Bauer suggested that the club put up one with an option for more. If the idea was good, people would support more. Hubka appointed a seven-person mural committee.

The results are in: "It exploded, and it's been absolutely amazing," committee member and art teacher Traci Lebo said.

The mural committee needed a name for the local community foundation's Match Day, when donations at a certain level are doubled by the sponsoring organization. Hubka chose A Mural Movement to put them at the top of the list. Match Day generated $15,000 in donations. And that was only the start.

The first project was *K-15 Mural*, a collection of Kansas license plates forming a K-15 sign, chosen because Clay Center is on Highway 15. Soon, the city featured a *Greetings from Clay Center* postcard. Key Feeds turned its elevator into *Bucolic America*. A red barn and windmill stand tall in a big blue sky, while a calf stands close to its mother in a lush green field. In two years, the movement has turned Clay Center into an outdoor art extravaganza.

Key Feeds

Christian and Jessica Stanley of C. Stanley Creative painted the 25th mural, the 2,080-square-foot *Sunflower State of Mind*. The couple lives in Orlando, Florida, but Jessica comes from Central Kansas. "It is fantastic to be in Kansas and painting," Jessica said. "This project is . . . meaningful to me and a great fit for us."

Clay Center doesn't intend to stop at 25. And that's how to paint the town.

The four murals in Marysville's Pony Express Plaza are unlike any other murals. Their scenes change as viewers walk past them. Each mural has 90 individual ribbed glass tiles with embedded images.

OUT OF THE BOX

Who turned cardboard into an art medium?

"Growing up impoverished in Northern Mexico, I had to create my own toys and items of amusement. This was the beginning of my creative bent."

—Jessie Montes

Jesus "Jessie" Montes was the sole survivor of five sets of twins. His mother taught him to read and write, but he didn't attend school. He emigrated from Mexico as a child and became a naturalized citizen in 1972.

By 1990, Montes was working as a Dodge City school custodian. When two of his children went to fight in the First Gulf War, Montes needed something to quell his anxiety for their safety. Since school districts receive lots of cardboard boxes, looking at the range of box sizes and thicknesses inspired Jessie to create outsider art.

Montes had never had art training, but "one day I just started cutting cardboard," he said. He recycled the free, plentiful supply of boxes and bulletin board papers. A picture frame for his son's photograph became his first project.

The frame started a unique art form. At first, Montes created two-dimensional art. Then he began to sculpt in three dimensions. From a distance, his art looks like woodcarving. Instead, Montes sliced cardboard into quarter-inch strips to expose the corrugation. Different angled cuts

JESSIE MONTES

WHAT: An artist in cardboard

WHERE: Duane and Orvileta West Council Service Center, 402 Fulton St., Garden City

COST: Free

PRO TIP: In 2017, the Wests donated their 53-piece Montes collection to the Boy Scouts' Santa Fe Trail Council. The service center's gallery displays their collection.

Buffalo Jones *by Jessie Montes*

Charles J. (Buffalo) Jones
First Mayor of Garden City
by Jessie "Jessie" M. Montes
using corrugated paper board (cardboard) & acrylics

Donated in December, 2000
by Duane & Orvileta West
friends and agents of the artist.

provided additional textures and colors. "That's what the secret is—the corrugated part. It creates the illusion of texture. That's where the art is," Montes said. He constructed his sculptures with tweezers, a sharp razor blade, acrylic paint, and paste. His work is brilliant, skilled, and supremely inventive.

Duane and Orvileta West purchased 25 of Montes's artworks in 1998. Then they became his agents. He exhibited his work in 24 venues in seven states. Two national art publications featured him.

Montes died in 2013. By the end of his life, his works brought $2,000 to $5,000 apiece.

Icarus, the man who flew too close to the sun with wax wings, is Montes's favorite. In Montes's art, an arrow always pierces Icarus's side. The mythological character "represents the desire to be free," but the arrow shows "that there's always something holding you back."

MARRIED TO ADVENTURE

What made Martin and Osa Johnson famous?

Martin Johnson of Independence convinced *Call of the Wild* author Jack London to let him sail around the globe as a cook on the *Snark*. Neither the Londons nor the ship spanned the globe, but Martin did. He became hooked on adventure.

Osa Leighty was 16 when Martin returned to Chanute in 1909. She attended one of his lectures about his *Snark* experiences, but she thought that he was conceited. Continued contact with Martin changed her opinion, and they eloped on May 15, 1910.

After seven years of fundraising, the Johnsons sailed to present-day Vanuatu and the Solomon Islands. On Malakula Island, Nagapate of the Big Namba tribe seized them. Then a British gunboat appeared and Nagapate released them. The adventure became the movie *Cannibals of the South Seas*.

They returned to the island in 1919 with an armed escort, but it turned out to be unnecessary. The tribe enjoyed seeing themselves on the big screen. *Cannibals* was the first of numerous movies, books, and other projects on which the couple collaborated. The

Johnsons went on to invent the wildlife documentary.

They each obtained their pilot's licenses in 1932. She flew in a zebra-striped plane named *Osa's Ark*. Martin named his giraffe-spotted plane *Spirit of Africa*. Together they logged 60,000 miles during their 1933–34 African excursion. The resulting film *Baboona* became the first in-flight movie.

After spending 1936 in Borneo, the couple returned to the US for a lecture tour. On January 12, 1937, their charter pilot crashed into a mountainside 16 miles from the Burbank, California, airport. Martin died the next day.

Even though the crash badly injured her, Osa continued their life's work. Her 1940 memoir, *I Married Adventure*, became a bestseller. Television's first wildlife program, Osa Johnson's *The Big Game Hunt*, premiered in 1952. She was planning a trip to East Africa when she died of a heart attack in 1953.

MARTIN AND OSA JOHNSON

WHAT: Pioneering travel journalists

WHERE: Martin and Osa Johnson Safari Museum, 111 N Lincoln Ave., Chanute

COST: Adults $6, seniors and students 13-college $4, children 6-12 $3, under 6 free with adult admission.

PRO TIP: Visit the outdoor mobile A *Flight into History* at E Main St. and S Santa Fe Ave. It honors aviation pioneer and Chanute namesake Octave Chanute.

Osa's mother, Ruby (Taylor) Leighty; Martin's sister, Freda (Johnson) Cripps; and the Chanute Chamber of Commerce opened the Martin and Osa Johnson Safari Museum in 1961. The museum highlights the Johnsons' and other explorers' achievements. Plus, it features an impressive art and artifact collection.

CLIMBING THE LEARNING TREE

What is Fort Scott's connection to Gordon Parks?

"You're to let this place be your learning tree. Trees bear good fruit and bad fruit, and that's the way it is here. Remember that."

—Sarah (Ross) Parks

Gordon Parks was the youngest of Andrew Jackson and Sarah (Ross) Parks's 15 children. He attended an integrated grade school in Fort Scott, but Black children could not play sports or attend social activities.

His mother died when he was 14. His father sent him to live with his sister Margaret in St. Paul, Minnesota, but Parks and his brother-in-law Edward Robinson did not get along. After an argument, Robinson banned Parks from their home— during a Minnesota winter.

After some hard times, Parks became a waiter on the North Coast Limited train. The photographs in the passengers' magazines inspired him, and in 1937 he purchased a camera in a pawnshop for $7.50. Parks later became the first Black photographer to work for *Life* and *Vogue* magazines.

Life sent Parks back to Fort Scott in 1950. Unfortunately, the magazine never published "Fort Scott Revisited," for unknown reasons. In 1963, he published a semi- autobiographical novel, *The Learning Tree*, about growing up Black in Fort Scott. The movie version made him Hollywood's first Black director. He also composed the film's score. The Library of Congress added the film to the National Film Registry in 1989.

"Like souls touching, poetry, music, paint, and the camera keep calling, and I can't bring myself to say no," he said.

Kansas State University awarded Parks an honorary doctorate in 1970. In 1985, the Native Sons and Daughters

GORDON PARKS

WHAT: Multifaceted Black author, musician, and film maker

WHERE: Gordon Parks Museum, Fort Scott Community College, 2108 S Horton St., Fort Scott

COST: Donation

PRO TIP: The museum developed the *Learning Tree* Film Scene and Sign Trail. Hundreds of people from Fort Scott and Mound City appeared as extras and a few had speaking roles in the film.

of Kansas named him Kansan of the Year. In 2006, the University of Kansas gave him the William Allen White Foundation National Citation. Parks said he had received many awards, but this one topped the list. "It's from Kansas," he said.

Parks died a month after his White award. He willed a large collection to the Gordon Parks Museum in Fort Scott. The museum's re-creation of his New York apartment includes his piano, desk, and sofa. His director's chair and movie camera are off to the side. It looks so realistic that visitors half expect that Parks will enter at any moment.

SURROUNDED BY ART

What is *Man Lying on a Platform* looking for?

The white Nerman Museum of Contemporary Art already stands out from the red brick buildings of Johnson County Community College (JCCC). The unbalanced second floor with a single window looks like Cyclops is bending over to search the surroundings. The structure leaves no doubt about its identity as a repository of art. Architect Kyu Sung Woo designed the two-level minimalist building covered in Kansas limestone.

As dusk falls, Leo Villareal's *Microcosm* comes to life above the front door. Fireflies spread throughout the overhang's ceiling, morphing into constellations of white light.

On the second floor, Do Ho Suh shaped *Some/One* like a traditional Asian armor coat. The armor plates comprise 3,000 misprinted military dog tags. The installation's back faces the door, so visitors see it first from behind. The tags crunch under viewers' feet as they circle the sculpture. The front is hollow and filled with mirrors, like looking into another dimension.

Stephan Balkenhol's *Man Lying on a Platform* is an impressionist painting rendered into sculpture. The brown-haired man wears a white shirt, dark pants, and brown shoes. He is resting on his elbow, watching something

---

NERMAN MUSEUM OF CONTEMPORARY ART

WHAT: Johnson County Community College's art museum

WHERE: Johnson County Community College, 12345 College Blvd., Overland Park

COST: Free

PRO TIP: Park in any open lot on campus or at the shopping center across the street. Reserve guided tours from Tuesdays through Saturdays between 10 a.m. and 4 p.m.

unknown. Balkenhol did not smooth his chisel strokes, so perhaps his work is waiting for unfinished business.

The Jerry and Margaret Nerman family donated the lead gift in 2003 to construct the museum. Then Marti and Tony Oppenheimer decided to establish the museum's permanent collection. They have donated more than 150 pieces of art, seeking to introduce art to students who might not normally come to a museum. "And now they are surrounded by art," Tony Oppenheimer said.

JCCC's $10 million art collection spreads all over campus. The most famous is *Walking Man (On the Edge)*, who strides precariously along the College Commons Building roof's edge.

Nerman Museum of Contemporary Art, Johnson County Community College. Courtesy of Timothy Hursley

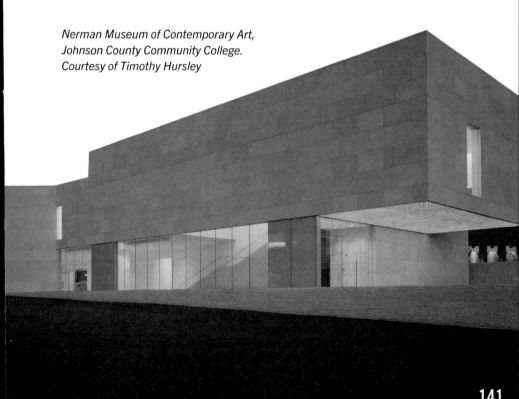

WHERE FASHION SITS

Where is the Johnson County Community College Fashion Collection?

> "Fashion is the mirror of history. It reflects political, social and economic changes, rather than mere whimsy." —Louis XIV

Imagine stepping into your fashionista friend's closet. You're about to play dress-up for grown-ups. You want a surprise, so you close your eyes and grab a garment. You open your eyes, and the closet is now 875 square feet and packed with gorgeous clothes. Mannequins strike a pose. Designer dresses hang from the racks, and boxed accessories are stacked on the rooms' walls. You blink in shocked delight.

That closet could have been a portal into the Johnson County Community College (JCCC) Fashion Collection. One room arranges clothes by decade. You examine the 1850s outfits and marvel at how small they were. The 1940s military style becomes Christian Dior's New Look. No doubt which clothes belong to the 1960s. Look, there's a pair of go-go boots! Oh, and there's the glittering, glamorous 1980s!

The other room holds designer clothes. American designers include Adrian, Irene, Nelly Dons, Norman Norell, Pauline Trigerie, Geoffrey Beene, and Bill Blass.

If your friend's closet portal permits, tune it to the Historic Costume and Textile Museum at Kansas State University, or call 785-532-6993 for a tour.

Dior, Coco Chanel, and Pierre Cardin represent the French couture.

In the 1970s, Jeanne Mathews started collecting fashion history. Her Jones Store clientele donated their retired clothing. JCCC's fashion department inherited Mathews's collection in the 1990s.

The 1950 American Royal Queen Mary Ellen (Ash) Rixey modeled at regional department stores. "She would be outstandingly happy that . . . some of these dresses could . . . be shown . . . for another 50 years, 80 years, 100, however long it takes," her son Norton Rixey said upon donating her things to JCCC.

Sometimes, items from the several-thousand-piece collection are loaned out as props, like holiday party dresses for the All-Electric House in the Johnson County Museum or exhibitions at the Nerman Museum on campus.

The fashion department dreams of a day when their collection itself becomes a museum. Put on the Ritz!

THE LAST PIECE OF KANZAS

What is the Unknown Indian Monument?

The State of Kansas derives its name from the Kanza (Kaánze níkashinga) tribe, the People of the South Wind. Unfortunately, the tribe lost its homeland and moved to Oklahoma in 1873.

Chief Allegawaho opposed the move. "You chase us to one stream, then you chase us to another," he said. "Soon, you will chase us over the mountains and into the ocean, and we will have no place to live." He demanded a higher price for the tribal lands but got nowhere. He died in Oklahoma around 1887.

August Haucke obtained some of the Kaánze níkashinga's land southeast of Council Grove. In August 1924, Boy Scouts discovered a tribal member's exposed remains. Out of respect to the exiled tribe, August's son Frank Haucke hired stonemasons to build a 35-foot-tall limestone obelisk and named it the Unknown Indian Monument.

Two thousand people came to lay the warrior to rest on August 12, 1925. A military band led a procession. Then, a squadron of soldiers guarded a caisson carrying a flag-draped copper casket. A Kaánze níkashinga led a riderless horse, followed by 25 Kaánze níkashingas on horseback. A troop of the Second US Cavalry from Fort Riley followed.

UNKNOWN INDIAN MONUMENT

WHAT: Memorial honoring a Kaánze níkashinga warrior

WHERE: Allegawaho Heritage Memorial Park, S 525 Rd., Council Grove

COST: Free

PRO TIP: Visitors are asked not to approach the monument any closer than the paved trail. The park is open during daylight hours.

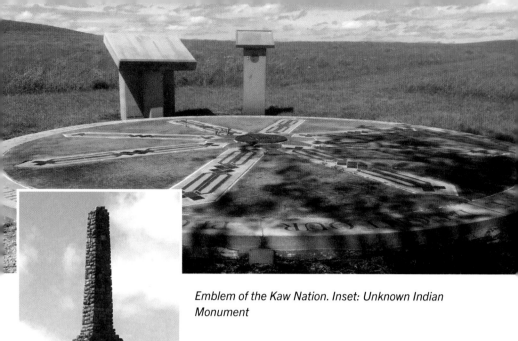

Emblem of the Kaw Nation. Inset: Unknown Indian Monument

After the interment, Allegawaho's grandson Roy Taylor spoke. "We dedicate this fine monument as the resting place of the unknown Indian. . . . When we return to our Oklahoma reservation, we will tell of your great kindness. We will not forget." The tribe adopted Haucke and renamed him Ga-he-gah-skeh, "White Chief."

In 2000, the Kaá^{n}ze níkashi^{n}ga purchased 168 acres around the monument to create Allegawaho Heritage Memorial Park. The land includes a sizeable tribal emblem marker, the Kaw (or Kanza) Agency ruins, and the remnants of a village. Although the government built stone houses for the Kaá^{n}ze níkashi^{n}ga, they preferred tribal-style homes, so the houses became stables.

The Kaá^{n}ze níkashi^{n}ga revere a massive red boulder, I^n 'zhúje 'waxóbe (Sacred Red Rock), at the mouth of Shunganunga Creek near present-day Tecumseh. The stone later became a monument to the pioneers in Robinson Park. The City of Lawrence agreed in 2022 to relocate the stone to Allegawaho Park.

THE GREAT SETTLEMENT AND THE LAST CONQUISTADOR

Where is Etzanoa?

Rumors about Quivira, one of the Seven Cities of Cibola, lured Francisco Vasquez de Coronado into Kansas in 1541. They were only a fable. Instead, he found the ancestors of the Kitikiti'sh (Wichita tribe).

Sixty years after Coronado's expedition, Juan de Oñate y Salazar, the Last Conquistador, sought Quivira again. He didn't find Quivira, but he did find Etzanoa, the Great Settlement, in 1601.

Before Oñate reached Etzanoa, its enemies tried to persuade the Spanish to attack. The explorers called them "Excanxaques." Instead, the Spanish and an Etzanoan delegation agreed to meet peacefully. The explorers then betrayed their agreement and took hostages, including the leader, Caratax. Seeing this, the settlement evacuated.

The Excanxaques tried to loot Etzanoa, but Oñate prevented them.

The explorers examined the city for three days. It occupied five miles on both sides of the Walnut River, and they estimated that 20,000 people lived there. Etzanoa was the second-largest

Potential Battle of Etzanoa site

North American settlement at the time. It was larger than present-day Arkansas City.

The looters returned, but the expedition repelled the warriors with guns and a cannon. They took cover in a rock-lined ditch as the soldiers peppered them with bullets. Many Excanxaques died in the battle but no Spaniards were killed.

The post-expedition report included maps showing Etzanoa's location, which mystified archaeologists for centuries. Eventually, Dr. Don Blakeslee of Wichita State University connected the report and previous archaeology surveys. He determined that Etzanoa had to be beneath present-day Arkansas City. In 2020, a drone survey found additional evidence to support Blakeslee's claim. Ark City residents were unsurprised. They had been finding artifacts since the city's 1870 founding.

Gary McAdams, the Kitikiti'sh Cultural Program Planner, hoped that, as a result of these findings, his "ancestors may finally receive their due for . . . [establishing their] great civilization . . . in the present state of Kansas during the 14th and 15th centuries."

ETZANOA

WHAT: A lost city

WHERE: Cherokee Strip Land Rush Museum, 31639 Hwy. 77, Arkansas City

COST: $10 for individual tours

PRO TIP: Book the 2.5-hour tours in advance. They start at the Cherokee Strip Land Rush Museum, and guests follow the tour guide in their own vehicles.

Blakeslee believes the Spaniards and Excanxaques fought the Battle of Etzanoa near what is now Walnut Park at 1100 E Madison Ave., Arkansas City. The Excanxaques's tribal identity is uncertain. The Etzanoans eventually freed Caratax and other hostages. However, the Spaniards kept the hostage boys to instruct them in the Catholic faith.

A REFUGE FAR FROM HOME

Which El Quartelejo tale is true?

Pioneers Herbert and Eliza Steele settled beside Scott County's Ladder Creek. One day, Herbert saw a prairie dog digging dried corn from a mound. He notified the Kansas State Historical Society. Soon Dr. Samuel W. Williston and Prof. Handel T. Martin came to investigate.

They discovered a buried pueblo with pottery and piles of corn. Further expeditions discovered the remains of buildings and irrigation ditches, once the pueblo of El Quartelejo.

Scholars have revealed divergent stories about El Quartelejo's history. In 1540, Conquistador Francisco Vasquez de Coronado discovered that the Seven Cities of Cibola were poorer than reported. He enslaved its people anyway.

The Puebloans revolted against Spanish rule in 1680. Luis and Lorenzo Tupatu murdered a priest and burned the San Lorenzo de Picuris Mission in New Mexico. Luis later became the Puebloan leader. When the Spaniards reestablished control 12 years later, the Picuris tribe (Pin, wel, ene) escaped to their Kansas refuge.

EL QUARTELEJO

WHAT: A potential refuge from slavery

WHERE: Historic Lake Scott State Park, 101 W Scott Lake Dr., Scott City

COST: State park permit

PRO TIP: The Northern Tsis tsis'tas (Cheyenne) fought the US Army in the 1878 Battle of Punished Woman's Fork at Battle Canyon south of the park. Also, visit the El Cuartelejo Museum/Jerry Thomas Gallery in Scott City.

The Spanish governor ordered Juan de Ulibarrí to recapture the tribe in 1706 to rescue them from the Apache tribe (Diné's) enslavement. De Ulibarrí's report said the Pin, wel, ene had "cried for joy" when he came to El Quartelejo. He "comforted" Lorenzo by saying the governor had ordered him to return all the members to Spanish control. If the Spanish account is believable, the Pin, wel, ene had only switched masters. However, Pin, wel, ene tradition says they had lived happily with the Diné for 14 years.

Before their departure, the Spaniards gave the "delighted" Diné "many good gifts." Sixty-seven Pin, wel, ene "who were living as apostate slaves" returned to New Mexico. Ulibarrí bragged about snaring Lorenzo and his nephew, Luis's son Juan Tupatu, "two of the most noteworthy Indians of the entire kingdom."

When the expedition arrived at San Lorenzo de Picuris Mission, the priest absolved the tribe from its apostasy. "It was a day of the greatest rejoicing this kingdom has ever seen," de Ulibarrí said.

Was the tribe rejoicing—or not?

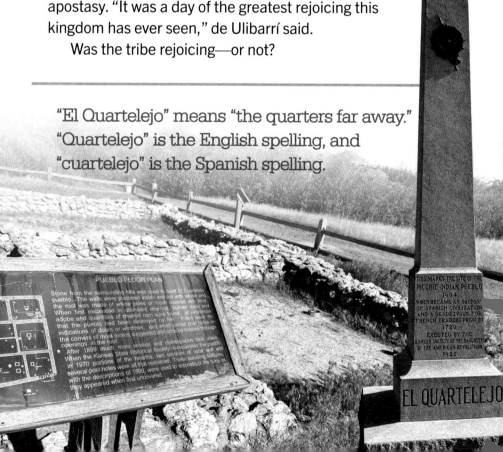

"El Quartelejo" means "the quarters far away." "Quartelejo" is the English spelling, and "cuartelejo" is the Spanish spelling.

PUEBLO FLOOR PLAN
Stone from the surrounding hills was used to build El Quartelejo pueblo. The walls were plastered inside and out with adobe and the roof was made of willow poles or brush covered with mud. When first excavated in abundant charcoal, burned tools and adobe and quantities of charred corn were found. All evidence that the pueblo had been destroyed by fire. There were no indications of doors or windows, and small paired post holes in the corners of most rooms suggested entrance by ladders through openings in the roof.
• After 1899 much more erosion and disintegration took place. When the Kansas State Historical Society re-excavated the pueblo in 1970 portions of the hearths, two sections of outer wall and several post holes were all that remained. These surviving features with the descriptions of 1899, were used to reconstruct the ruins as they appeared when first uncovered.

THIS MARKS THE SITE OF THE PICURIE INDIAN PUEBLO 1664 WHICH BECAME AN OUTPOST OF SPANISH CIVILIZATION AND A RENDEZVOUS FOR FRENCH TRADERS PRIOR TO 1720 ERECTED BY THE KANSAS SOCIETY OF THE DAUGHTERS OF THE AMERICAN REVOLUTION 1935

EL QUARTELEJO

FROM SACRED TO SUBMERGED

What happened to Waconda Spring?

"Nothing will ever replace the wondrous heritage that we now prepare to destroy." —*Salina Journal*, April 25, 1965

Waconda Spring has brought spiritual and physical benefits to visitors for centuries. Then the Glen Elder Dam capped and buried it. Eventually, the spring's friends built a replica to honor its memory.

Long before the dam was built, the Kanza (Kaánze níkashinga) named the spring "Wakonda," which means "Great Spirit." The Pawnee bathed in the spring to purify themselves. The other area tribes also revered the spring, and conflict was forbidden there.

After the indigenous people were gone, a bottling company sold Waconda Water nationwide. The spring's water mainly contained sodium chloride and sodium sulfide, with magnesium and various carbonates. Its success inspired an on-site hotel and spa.

Three generations of the Abrahams/Bingesser family ran the spa. Waconda Water "will clean your works until your works work," Dr. Carlos Bingesser quipped. Thousands of people "cleaned their works" each year.

The Great Flood of 1951 jammed up Bingesser's plans. Downtown Manhattan drowned beneath six feet of water. Other downstream cities suffered similarly, and they cried for protection. The Bureau of Reclamation decided to build a dam that would protect the cities but would require submerging the spring. Bingesser and others fought the bureau. A hydrologist who was brought in to inspect the spring declared it was unique in the world.

WACONDA SPRING

WHAT: A drowned mineral spring

WHERE: Waconda Visitor & Education Center, Glen Elder State Park, 2131 180 Rd., Glen Elder

COST: State park permit

PRO TIP: The visitors center holds a mural depicting the Legend of Wakonda. Also, see memorabilia like "Waconda Waltz" sheet music and a Waconda Water ceramic jug.

Instead, the dam's proponents derided the spring as a "mud hole." The bureau claimed the spring water would "contaminate" the lake. Eventually, the Bureau capped the spring, demolished Bingesser's buildings, and dropped the debris atop the springs. Between 1968 and 1970, Waconda Spring became Waconda Lake, and what had once been sacred was submerged.

The Waconda Heritage Association dedicated a half-sized spring replica in 2005. The Waconda Cultural Association repaired the reproduction, added interpretive signage, and placed a buoy above the spring's location in the lake.

A legend says that Wakonda fell in love with Takota from an enemy tribe. When they asked permission to marry, one of her father's warriors shot him. He fell into the spring and Wakonda jumped in. She never resurfaced. The tribes believed that her spirit remained in the spring.

THE LAST KANSAS RESERVOIR

What does it take to build a lake?

Federal agencies built 28 Kansas dams in 33 years, and then the dam building stopped. Later, however, the dam builders got one more chance.

In 1953, Kansas enacted the Watershed District Act. As a result, portions of Southwest Kansas formed the Pawnee Watershed District. The 1.5-million-acre district is the nation's largest. It would eventually construct Horsethief Reservoir behind the state's last dam.

The district filed its water rights application for the Horsethief Reservoir on September 17, 1985. District Manager Ron Allen led the project. During the next 10 years, the district held hearings and addressed concerns. "Everybody said [the reservoir] would never fill with water," Manager Audrey Rupp recalled.

Another eight years passed while engineers designed the dam, and the district sought funding. The legislature said the Horsethief Reservoir Benefit District could levy a sales tax in 2004. Consequently, Hodgeman, Ford, Gray, and Finney counties' citizens approved the tax 2−1.

HORSETHIEF RESERVOIR

WHAT: The newest Kansas reservoir

WHERE: Horsethief Reservoir, 19005 SW Hwy. 156, Jetmore

COST: Daily vehicle fees are $5. Check the website for additional fees.

PRO TIP: Horsethief is not a state park, so state permits are invalid. Follow all Kansas fishing and boating license requirements and reservoir regulations.

Sunrise at Horsethief Reservoir

At last, 23 years after they applied, the district broke ground nine miles west of Jetmore. MJE LLC of Montezuma completed the 7,200-foot dam in 2009. The lake began to fill on September 8, 2009. The reservoir, dam, and the surrounding park took shape together.

By the spring of 2010, the reservoir was half full. It reached capacity on July 1, 2016. The 450-acre reservoir is the largest water body in Southwest Kansas. The reservoir allowed limited boating and fishing in June 2010 and camping two years later. In 2018, 100,000 visitors enjoyed the park.

Horsethief offers boating, fishing, swimming, archery, hunting, trails, and camping. The camping options include five yurts. Two of them have all the comforts of home.

That's what it takes to make a champion lake.

Sadly, Allen died on July 4, 2010. His final illness prevented him from enjoying Opening Weekend. Honor his memory at the Ron Allen Memorial Disc Golf Course.

TO THE GLORY OF GOD

What is Damar's chief treasure?

Today, the twin spires adorning St. Joseph Catholic Church, Damar, appear above the horizon for miles before travelers reach the little city in northwestern Rooks County. The city's street signs include the church's silhouette.

Families from the St. Peter's community staked claims near present-day Damar in 1877, and other French-Canadian Catholics followed. The parish priests said Mass in French until 1923.

By 1912, Damar had outgrown its church, so the Peter Simoneau family donated land for a new structure. The parish and Father S. F. Guillaume planned a Richardsonian Romanesque edifice. Architect Henry W. Brinkman of Emporia designed a building 128 feet long and 72 feet wide at the transepts.

The parish laid St. Joseph's cornerstone in 1912, but finances forced them to work in stages. The exterior limestone came from a quarry in Waldo. With the parishioners doing most of the work, the church towers arose in 1913. One stage finished the interior decoration. Another added pews and a heating system. By 1952, 40 years after breaking ground, the church had a copper roof, interior decoration, and antique European stained-glass windows.

ST. JOSEPH CATHOLIC CHURCH

WHAT: An exquisite Northwest Kansas church

WHERE: 107 Oak St., Damar

COST: Donation

PRO TIP: Contact the Damar Visitors Center, 785-726-3540, for tours.

The slow process produced spectacular results. For example, alternating blue and old gold strips cover the apse. Three gold leaf stripes adorn each block, with fleur de lis and crowns on the stripes. On the dome above, angel paintings adore the triumphant Lamb of God. Filigreed designs surround the Lamb. The crucifix hangs below an elaborate double arch with stylized golden grapes, wheat sheaves, and maroon maple leaves on the wall. The nave's 34 gypsum columns used the painstaking scagliola plastering process to look like marble.

When the church's roof began to leak, Damar refused to give up its church. They raised $300,000 to return it to its former magnificence in 2007 for the glory of God and the pride of Damar.

If the weather cooperates, order a meal to go at Dad's Place/Damar Café. Then drive 15 minutes on scenic Highway 24 to Webster State Park for a picnic lunch.

PROMISE KEPT

Who was Phillip Colleton?

A severe thunderstorm pelted Father Phillip Colleton in 1869. The priest vowed to build a church at that spot if he lived through the storm. However, the promised site was in the Neutral Strip, created to isolate the Cherokees from white encroachment. Titles were tangled, and settlers weren't coming.

Colleton was a Jesuit missionary based at Osage Mission in St. Paul. He helped the mission design one of its first school buildings. He stocked the building's library and devised a way to distribute religious material to area Catholics.

Two years after the storm, Colleton had fulfilled his promise with the completion of Crawford County's first church in a small wooden building beside the Historic Mission Road at present-day Greenbush. Colleton also started eight other area churches and helped start some Catholic schools as well.

The railroads enabled the Osage Mission priests to extend their ministries. While trail riding was rough, railroads were hazardous, too. Colleton survived two train wrecks.

However, on January 16, 1876, Colleton took a six-mile trip from Parsons to Ladore on a railroad handcart. The pump bar struck him in the chest, the impact knocked him into a toolbox, and he fell unconscious. The accident killed him 11 months later after an apparent hemorrhage.

ST. ALOYSIUS CATHOLIC CHURCH

WHAT: Crawford County's first church

WHERE: 947 Hwy. 47, Girard

COST: Free

PRO TIP: St. Aloysius Historical Society holds an annual Greenbush Day. Visit the grotto's Nativity scene at Christmastime.

St. Aloysius Church

The following year, another storm destroyed the Greenbush church. The parishioners quarried stone from Hickory Creek limestone and finished a new church in 1881. In 1907, the church dedicated a larger stone building, and the second church became a community center. Then, in 1982, lightning struck the third church.

Undeterred, the parish returned to the second church, which technically became the parish's fourth church. Unfortunately, the Diocese of Wichita closed nine Southeast Kansas churches, including St. Aloysius, in 1993. The parish installed a grotto of the Blessed Virgin Mary in the 1907 church's ruins and the 1881 church is now a community center. Father Colleton's promise lives on.

Learn more about Southeast Kansas Jesuit priests at the Osage Mission Neosho County Museum in St. Paul. Colleton rests in the St. Francis Cemetery there.

TREATS WITHOUT TRICKS

Who started Hiawatha's Halloween Frolic?

After Halloween 1914, Elizabeth Krebs surveyed the damage to the flower garden that had consoled her after she lost three adult children in three years. Distressed, she resolved to end Hiawatha's Night of Destruction. "I could not bear having our orderly homes become the playthings for thoughtless and mischief-loving youths," she recalled.

She went to Hiawatha's Civic Improvement Club and suggested that they establish "a sane Halloween" in 1915. People called her foolish, but she persisted. Eventually, she convinced the owners of the *Hiawatha Daily World* to promote a supervised Halloween event. They induced the business community to offer prizes for the best costumes. A band and nearly 200 costumed children paraded through Hiawatha's streets. While thousands of spectators watched, the judges awarded prizes at the opera house afterward. The

Courtesy of the Hiawatha Halloween Frolic

Holton Recorder said Krebs's idea "was a clever one, and every town should adopt the plan."

The event kept growing. In 1919, Hiawatha crowned Ruth Rice as the first Halloween Carnival Queen. Her crowning was more dramatic than organizers desired. The lights went out as soon as she sat on her throne. Fixing them took some time on a cold night.

When the curtain finally went up, "my fiancé, Frank Sterns, was very surprised to see that the queen was 'his girl,'" the queen recalled. "My father said, 'I've been standing half froze, and I see that girl every day at home!'"

Hiawatha cherishes their event as the nation's oldest organized Halloween event. Now it includes two big parades, contests with trophies and cash prizes, and the queen contest.

HIAWATHA HALLOWEEN FROLIC

WHAT: A sane Halloween

WHERE: Hiawatha

COST: Free

PRO TIP: Check the Hiawatha Halloween Frolic Facebook page for event details.

When Halloween falls on a weekday, Hiawatha cancels school. The schools free hundreds of costumed children to parade in the afternoon. The best costumes, decorated bikes, trikes, wagons, family floats, small motorized vehicles, and horses win prizes.

The evening's Grand Parade features dignitaries such as the Kansas governor and other political leaders, high school bands, floats, horses, Shrine units, and natives in costume.

Krebs died in 1931, but she is always the ceremonial grand marshal. A truck bearing a sign, "In Memory of Mrs. Krebs, Parade Founder," always leads both parades.

ELKHART'S OLYMPIC GLORY

What is the world's smallest county with two Olympic medalists?

"If you have endurance, you are bound to win over those who haven't."—Glenn Cunningham

Twenty years apart, two Morton County runners stood on Olympic medal podiums. Both overcame childhood injuries to become champions.

Glenn Cunningham finished fourth in the 1,500-meter run during the Los Angeles 1932 Summer Olympics and won a silver medal in the 1,500 four years later in Berlin.

Thane Baker won a silver medal in the 200-meter run during 1952's Olympics in Helsinki, Finland. Four years later, in Melbourne, Australia, he won a bronze in the 200, silver in the 100, and gold in the 4 by 100 relay.

Neither man's victories were easy.

One morning, Floyd and Glenn Cunningham started the school stove northeast of Winfield. Unfortunately, someone had filled the kerosene can with gasoline. When Floyd lit the fire, the stove exploded, killing him. Glenn survived, but doctors predicted he would never walk.

Two years later, Cunningham left his wheelchair and crawled to a fence. He pulled himself upright. For months, Cunningham forced his seemingly useless legs to work. He discovered that running hurt less than walking, so he ran.

Cunningham broke the high school mile record in his senior year at Elkhart. He then ran for the University of Kansas. Cunningham eventually retired with multiple NCAA and AAU championships. He'd set world records five times.

Metal pierced Thane Baker's left knee as a high school freshman, and surgeons could not remove the shard. The injury sidelined him for two years. He eventually joined the Kansas State University track team as a walk-on.

Baker added his own workout to his coach's practice plan. Teammate Dick Towers was Baker's "rabbit," pushing him. When he qualified for Helsinki, the people of Manhattan raised funds to send coach Ward Haylett as a spectator. Baker's 4 by 200 relay set a world record in 1956. He owned the 300-yard world record from 1956 to 1974.

James Bausch of Garden Plain won decathlon gold in 1932, setting a world record for points. Twenty years later, Kansas sent nine Olympians, including Baker, to the 1952 Games. Seven Kansas Jayhawks won basketball gold. Ashland's Wes Santee ran the 1,500 meters but unfortunately did not achieve a medal.

Thane Baker. Courtesy of Morton County Museum

A TETER THAT WON'T TOTTER

Who installed Teter Rock?

James Teter installed the initial Teter Rock to guide pioneers to homes in the Cottonwood River Valley. The Flint Hills could be confusing, and people often became lost. The guidepost rock ensured that they would find his land instead of losing time wandering beside the Verdigris River.

Teter's original rock was like a cairn, a pile of stones. Unfortunately, settlers "borrowed" the rocks for building material, and the guidepost soon disappeared. Teterville and other towns sprang up during the Kansas oil boom. The settlement held almost 1,000 people with two general stores, a post office, and an elementary school. Today, only Teterville's foundations remain with an old oil-heating tank watching over them.

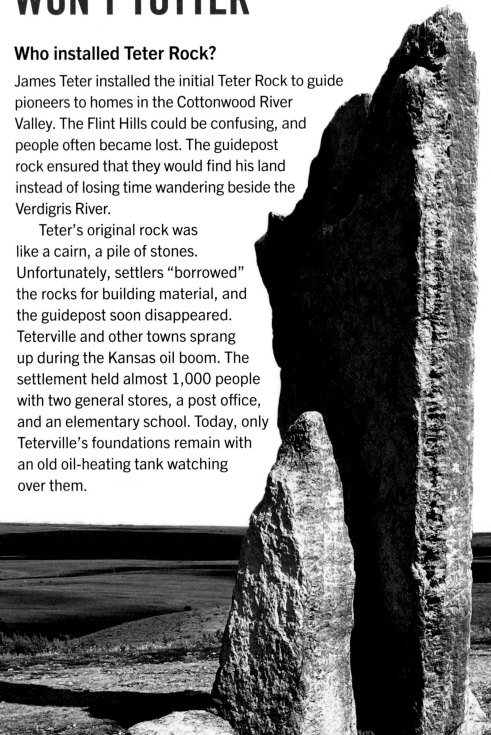

About 1954, J. Murle Teter, James's grandson, found a large limestone rock on his property. His equipment could not shift it, so he asked the Arapahoe Pipeline Company to lend him their equipment. With the company's help, Murle installed the rock as a monolith on a promontory to honor his grandfather. The slab extends six feet down and 16 feet in the air.

Some people say the rock looks like a howling wolf. Others say it's a giant shock of wheat or maybe a partially buried bone. Four counties, Woodson, Elk, Butler, and Chase, are visible from the hill. Wild horses may be grazing within sight. Deer, antelope, and other wildlife also inhabit the area. The Flint Hills are a haven for cattle.

A map app will likely get you to the rock's turnoff and recommend an uphill hike. However, a field road does lead to the monolith. A low-clearance car can make the trip cautiously, but a high-clearance vehicle would be better. Prepare to dodge deep ruts and avoid the road in wet weather.

The view speckled with summer wildflowers is spectacular. Astrophotography buffs will enjoy shooting pictures of the stars.

For more vistas, visit Texaco Hill near Teter Rock. Pass the entrance to Teter Rock, then turn north onto a dirt field road until arriving atop Texaco Hill.

DIAMONDS ARE A HOTEL'S BEST FRIEND

Where is the Grand Central Hotel?

In the song "Carry On Wayward Son," Kerry Livgren and his Kansas bandmates escape from "the noise and confusion just to get beyond this illusion." The Grand Central Hotel in Cottonwood Falls helps guests escape noise and confusion, and that is not an illusion.

M. M. Young opened the Grand Central Hotel in 1884 to serve railroad passenger traffic. The hotel rotated through different names and owners. Its names included Central House, the American, and then the Cottonwood Falls Hotel.

The hotel eventually closed. It fell into disrepair during the 1980s and 1990s. Finally, a couple from Kansas City bought the hotel for $41 at a tax auction. The 10-room hotel reopened on November 17, 1995, with its name restored as the Grand Central Hotel. The first-floor restaurant added "Grill" to the facility's name with Suzan Barnes as the manager. After several more ownership changes, Barnes bought the hotel in 2002. The property has earned multiple AAA Four Diamond Awards. The hotel has "become a destination; that's what we wanted," Barnes said. "I knew there was a need for a place in the Flint Hills."

Register inside the front door. The bar and sitting area are on the left, with the dining area on the right. The rooms

---

THE GRAND CENTRAL HOTEL AND GRILL

WHAT: Top-notch Flint Hills hotel

WHERE: 215 Broadway St., Cottonwood Falls

COST: Varies per suite

PRO TIP: The hotel offers a continental breakfast in the morning but lacks an elevator.

are upstairs. Each door has a spur-shaped knocker and a historic ranch brand burned into a wood block. The rooms feature cowboy and Western artwork. Rooms have modern amenities, such as spa-style showers, flat-screen televisions, and single-serve coffeemakers.

Enjoy a premium steak and drinks in the first-floor Grand Central Grill in the evenings.

Every day in the Flint Hills offers an escape from noise and confusion. The Grand Central Hotel amplifies the Flint Hills' calming effect. Carry on, wayward son.

In 1996, the National Park Service opened the Tallgrass Prairie National Preserve five miles north of the hotel, but Chase County offers more than just the national preserve. Start by exploring at the ornate French Empire–design Chase County Courthouse at the south end of Broadway.

Grand Central Hotel

THE ULTIMATE MAN CAVE

What is hiding beneath Ellinwood's streets?

From 1887 until the early 1920s, Ellinwood had two communities, one above the ground and one below. Only men entered the labyrinth underneath the streets—the ultimate man cave. Cowboys and teamsters clustered below the ground.

However, the railroads replaced the teamsters, while quarantines and barbed wire pushed out the cowboys. Underground Ellinwood went with them. The city filled in most of the tunnels.

In 1979, Adrianna Dierolf inherited some downtown buildings. When she investigated her new property, she discovered the subterranean city. Purple tiles on the surface were skylights underground. Visitors may follow her explorer footsteps on the Ellinwood Underground Tour. The tour starts at Ellinwood Emporium's storeroom where explorers walk down a stairwell onto an uneven floor and into a dusty environment.

Tom Drake's Harness Shop is the first stop. It looks like Drake just left his tools and stepped out for a bit. While Drake fixed their mounts' tack and the laundress cleaned their clothes, the cowboys could get a haircut and play cards. Look for bullet holes in the walls.

Jung's Barbershop also offered tonsillectomies back in the day. To remove troublesome tonsils, the patient sat

The Wolf Hotel serves fried chicken, chicken-fried steak, and homemade pies on every third Sunday. Call for reservations.

open-mouthed in the barber's chair, holding a basin with a curved indentation on one side, which was tucked underneath the patient's chin. After the patient had downed a numbing shot of whiskey, the barber yanked out the offending organs with special tongs. Then the patient recovered in a wheelchair.

Renovations blocked the tunnel from the emporium to the Wolf Hotel, so today's guests need to cross the street on the surface, then proceed back down. The hotel had arranged its side of Underground Ellinwood as shops, including a dressmaker, a toy shop, and a jail. Despite the sign that says the bar is closed "for violation of the National Prohibition Act," these days the Underground serves Prohibition-era libations to celebrate its repeal.

Enjoy the sound of the Underground in Ellinwood.

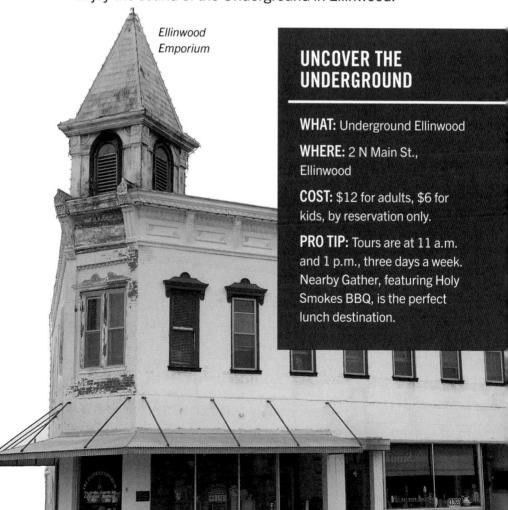

Ellinwood Emporium

UNCOVER THE UNDERGROUND

WHAT: Underground Ellinwood

WHERE: 2 N Main St., Ellinwood

COST: $12 for adults, $6 for kids, by reservation only.

PRO TIP: Tours are at 11 a.m. and 1 p.m., three days a week. Nearby Gather, featuring Holy Smokes BBQ, is the perfect lunch destination.

AMERICAN BANDSTAND

Which band west of the Mississippi has played the longest?

Dick Clark hosted popular music's top acts weekly for 37 years on *American Bandstand*. That's impressive, but the Iola Municipal Band has been playing for more than 150 years. It's the longest-tenured municipal band west of the Mississippi River.

The band fills the Allen County Courthouse Square's 1910 bandshell every summer. The concert begins each Thursday at 8 p.m. in June and July. The "Star-Spangled Banner" and a John Phillip Sousa tune start and end the evening.

Some band members have played for decades. Some are in middle school and high school. Director Jenna Morris tries to choose music that "we can play together and keep on with."

Several hundred people attend the performances, arriving much earlier than the 8 p.m. showtime. Some audience members listen from their parked cars. Others sit on park benches, blankets, and lawn chairs. Community organizations take turns serving ice cream and cake.

Iola incorporated in 1870. The following year, H. A. Needham and Col. Henry Talcott formed the Iola Silver Cornet Band. When World War I ended, the mayor called the band director at 2 a.m. The director picked up his horn and started marching around the town square. Within 15 minutes, the rest of the band members joined him. Half the

IOLA MUNICIPAL BAND

WHAT: The state's longest-tenured municipal band

WHERE: Allen County Courthouse Square, 1 W Madison Ave., Iola

COST: Free

PRO TIP: If you like the music, honk your car horn after the selection.

Courtesy of Iola Municipal Band

town came to listen and sing "Over There" and "Keep the Home Fires Burning."

The band still performs during Iola's Memorial Day celebration, so stop and listen to Iola's American bandstand.

While waiting for the concert, explore the town square.

SOURCES

A Life of Hope and Mercy
https://www.army.mil/standto/archive/2013/04/11/?; https://
www.youtube.com/watch?v=30UvI8BTEDQ; https://frkapaun.
org/; https://en.yna.co.kr/view/AEN20210727007900315;
https://hfpmc.org/churches/st-john-nepomucene-pilsen

A Hero Upgraded
https://roxieontheroad.com/jack-weinstein-medal-of-honor/;
https://www.findagrave.com/memorial/126741111/
jack-weinstein; https://www.youtube.com/
watch?v=_0tSmannMwU&t=3446s

Conley Sisters 1, Developers 0
https://www.kckpl.org/kansas/conley-sisters.html; https://
www.kckpl.org/kansas/articles/conley-family/1910-conley-v-
ballinger-supreme-court-opinion.pdf; https://www.findagrave.
com/memorial/6141270/eliza-conley; https://kchistory.org/
blog/lyda-conley-wyandot-guardian-and-lawyer; https://www.
wyandot.org/wyandotKS/huron-indian-cemetery-chronology/

Emancipation before Proclamation
https://civilwaronthewesternborder.org/encyclopedia/
quindaro-kansas; https://www.kckpl.org/kansas/quindaro.html;
https://www.kshs.org/kansapedia/quindaro/15163; https://
www.kansascity.com/news/your-kcq/article258753333.html;
https://kctoday.6amcity.com/quindaro-town-ruins-kansas-city-
ks-underground-railroad/

June Cleaver's Paradise
https://www.womenshistory.org/articles/defense-june-cleaver;
https://www.jcprd.com/933/1950s-All-Electric-House;
https://www.jcprd.com/1811/Special-Exhibit — -Redlined-
Cities-Suburb; https://dsl.richmond.edu/panorama/
redlining/#loc=14/39.015/-94.661&city=greater-kansas-city-
mo&area=B6; https://www.huduser.gov/portal/sites/default/
files/pdf/Federal-Housing-Administration-Underwriting-Manual.
pdf

Segregation Defeated
https://www.visitwichita.com/blog/post/dockum-drugstore-
sit-in-why-it-matters-to-wichitas-rich-cultural-history/;
https://www.npr.org/2006/10/21/6355095/kansas-sit-in-
gets-its-due-at-last; https://www.oklahoman.com/story/
business/2018/08/12/60-years-later-oklahomas-sit-in-
movement-is-remembered/60508097007/; https://www.
wichita.gov/ParkandRec/CityParks/Pages/ChesterILewis.aspx;
https://dockum.com/; https://www.loc.gov/exhibits/civil-rights-
act/epilogue.html

Segregación No Más
https://kansashistoricalsociety.newspapers.com/
clip/108523292/argentine-to-have-mexican-school/; https://
www.kshs.org/kansapedia/argentine-high-school/16694;
https://kckplprograms.org/2021/09/16/saturnino-alvarado/;
https://www.kshb.com/news/local-news/hispanic-heritage-
month/remembering-the-4-mexican-americans-who-
challenged-school-segregation-at-argentine-high-school;
https://www.kckcc.edu/foundation/events/hall-of-fame/index.
html

White vs. White Supremacy
https://www.kshs.org/p/william-allen-white-s-1924-
gubernatorial-campaign/13257; https://kansasreflector.
com/2020/10/31/when-real-american-william-allen-white-ran-
for-office-to-save-kansas-from-the-kkk/; https://www.kshs.
org/archives/440264; https://www.emporiagazette.com/news/
article_dd71e51c-f6dd-11e2-b41b-10604b9f6eda.html;
https://www.kshs.org/kansapedia/william-allen-white/16139;
https://kansasreflector.com/2021/10/17/nearly-a-century-
ago-a-kansas-mayor-was-brutalized-by-the-klan-todays-
rhetoric-sounds-chillingly-familiar/; https://www.kshs.org/p/
kansas-battles-the-invisible-empire/13247

Angel with a Blue Dress On
https://www.humanitieskansas.org/
doccenterSourcesa43c6d9b3982476aae2b61f62747c3
dfhttps://www.findagrave.com/memorial/102805633/
elizabeth-polly; https://www.findagrave.com/
cemetery/2478500/sentinel-hill; https://www.kshs.org/
publicat/khq/1971/1971winter_powers.pdf

Christy's Mystery
https://www.c2tranch.com/the-battle-of-the-saline-river;
hayspost.com/posts/de2e1cb1-7bea-4439-8b13-
337f1a00bf5c; https://valley.lib.virginia.edu/VoS/
personalpapers/documents/franklin/p2demusletters.
html; https://www.ancestry.com/discoveryui-content/
view/159470:1934?tid=&pid=&queryId=
0e8af419f873c323dc95fcb1261a6e7b&_phsrc=eJO4&_
phstart=successSource; https://www.ancestry.com/
discoveryui-content/view/161037:1934?tid=&pid=&queryId=
dbf6c49f3908d54e2b63538d8c4aa858&_phsrc=eJO31&_
phstart=successSource
Bigelow, Jr., John. "The Tenth Regiment of Cavalry." In The Army
of the United States: Historical Sketches of Staff and Line with
Portraits of Generals-in-Chief, edited by Theophilus Francis
Rodenbough,William Lawrence Haskin, 288-297. New York:
Maynard Merrill & Co., 1896.

Boxcar Full of Gratitude
https://www.patriotoutreach.org/docs/Merci_Boxcar_Flyer.pdf;
https://www.visithays.com/240/Kansas-Merci-Boxcar-Veterans-
Memorial-Pa; https://avedac.com/snapshots/2015/11-06-15.
htm; http://mercitrain.org/Kansas/; http://www.mercitrain.org/;
https://ameshistory.org/content/friendship-train-france;

Home of Veterans Day
https://visitemporia.com/emporians-lead-the-nation-
in-establishing-veterans-day/; https://kslib.info/Blog.
aspx?IID=880&ARC=1073; http://www.allveteransday.org/;
https://www.cmohs.org/recipients/grant-f-timmerman

Architect of the GI Bill
https://www.kshs.org/kansapedia/harry-walter-
colmery/16846; https://kansaslegion.org/345-2; https://
www.cjonline.com/story/news/local/2015/10/26/
harry-colmery-statue-honors-unsung-hero-american-
veterans/16612668007/; https://www.defense.gov/News/
Feature-Stories/story/Article/1727086/75-years-of-the-gi-bill-
how-transformative-its-been/; https://www.cjonline.com/story/
news/local/2020/08/26/history-guy-historical-statues-put-up-
in-recent-years-in-downtown-topeka/114912160/

Hear Us Roar

https://kansassampler.org/8wondersofkansas-people/amazon-army-crawford-county; http://www.franklinkansas.com/amazonarmy/amazonarmy%20-Knoll%20website/Index.html; https://portside.org/2021-11-21/amazon-army-and-1919-1922-kansas-coal-strikes; http://plainshumanities.unl.edu/encyclopedia/doc/egp.pd.003; https://www.kshs.org/kansapedia/amazon-army/16702; https://pplonline.org/about/

Infidelity

https://www.findagrave.com/memorial/32642058/william-h-windsor; https://www.findagrave.com/memorial/19005922/john-h-fry; https://usminedisasters.miningquiz.com/saxsewell/1916_Fidelity_No_9_Report.pdf; https://www.findagrave.com/memorial/32594627/lyrton-s-hey; https://kansashistoricalsociety.newspapers.com/clip/102175192/mayer-mine-to-resume; https://kansashistoricalsociety.newspapers.com/clip/102177089/20-miners-die-in-mine/; https://kansashistoricalsociety.newspapers.com/clip/102174359/stone-city-mine-disaster/; https://kansashistoricalsociety.newspapers.com/clip/102208425/relief-fund-growing/

Welcome to the Jungle

https://www.crf-usa.org/bill-of-rights-in-action/bria-24-1-b-upton-sinclairs-the-jungle-muckraking-the-meat-packing-industry.html; https://kansaspublicradio.org/kpr-news/little-blue-books-kansas-creation-celebrates-100-years; https://www.mtsu.edu/first-amendment/article/1063/red-scare; https://sites.google.com/site/girardchamber/about-us

The Ultimate Tax Protest

https://www.in2013dollars.com/us/inflation/1909?amount=84000; https://www.kshs.org/geog/geog_counties/view/county:GT; https://fhsuguides.fhsu.edu/kansasheritage/grantcounty; https://www.grantcoks.org/DocumentCenter/View/2746/Before-the-Move?bidId=

The Taxless Town

https://static1.squarespace.com/static/59ee165c7106998bfa7cc65b/t/5b5784476d2a73c04df20ffd/1532462152331/powerplant+%28WP%29.pdf; https://kansashistoricalsociety.newspapers.com/clip/107460257/vote-week-from-today-continued; https://kansashistoricalsociety.newspapers.com/clip/107460458/vote-week-from-today/; Miner, Craig. Harvesting the High Plains: John Kriss and the Business of Wheat Farming, 1920-1950. Lawrence, KS.: University Press of Kansas, 1998.

Less Corn and More Hell

https://www.kshs.org/p/kansas-historical-quarterly-the-disaffection-of-mary-elizabeth-lease/; https://dspacep01.emporia.edu/bitstream/handle/123456789/582/Gundersen%20Vol%2013%20Num%204.pdf?sequence=1; http://www.ksgenweb.org/archives/1912/l/lease_mary_elizabeth.html; https://www.acatholicmission.org/mary-elizabeth-lease.html; https://www.kansas.com/news/local/article1084885.html

To Spite Your Face

https://www.kshs.org/p/kansas-historical-quarterly-county-seat-controversies-in-southwestern-kansas/12569; https://kslib.info/835/Article-9-County-and-Township-Organizati; https://kansashistoricalsociety.newspapers.com/clip/102962378/goodbye-eminence-goodbye/; https://kansashistoricalsociety.newspapers.com/clip/102966891/432-vs-428/; https://archive.org/details/conquestofsouthw00blan; https://ccrsresearchcollections.omeka.net/items/show/181; Fitzgerald, Daniel. Ghost Towns of Kansas: A Traveler's Guide. University Press of Kansas, 1988.

A Dead Man for Breakfast

https://www.buffalobilloakley.org/cms/wp-content/uploads/Sheridan-Lawless-City-of-the-Plains.pdf; https://www.youtube.com/watch?v=ISFvQw5I-yg; https://www.kansasmemory.org/item/221562/page/17935; Fitzgerald, Daniel. Ghost Towns of Kansas: A Traveler's Guide. University Press of Kansas, 1988.

"Nobody There No How"

https://www.hutchnews.com/story/news/local/2014/04/18/cousin-eddie-s-coolidge/20909576007/; https://kansashistoricalsociety.newspapers.com/clip/107579377/the-sparrow-case/; https://www.facebook.com/trailcitybb; https://mynehistory.com/items/show/204?tour=3&index=38; Fitzgerald, Daniel. Ghost Towns of Kansas: A Traveler's Guide. University Press of Kansas, 1988.; Chrisman, Harry E.. Ladder of Rivers: The Story of I.P. "Print" Olive, Chicago: Sage Books, 1983.

Never Runs Dry

http://worldfamousgunfighters.weebly.com/cheyenne-exodus.html; https://www.kshs.org/publicat/history/1984autumn_powers.pdf; https://naturalatlas.com/geologic-formations/big-basin-formation-2769889; https://ksoutdoors.com/KDWP-Info/Locations/Wildlife-Areas/Southwest/Big-Basin-Prairie-Preserve; https://geokansas.ku.edu/big-basin-and-little-basin; https://ksoutdoors.com/Fishing/Where-to-Fish-in-Kansas/Fishing-Locations-Public-Waters/Southwest-Region/Clark-State-Fishing-Lake

No Bull

http://www.hwy24.org/uploads/2/6/1/8/26189167/28_town_names.pdf; https://www.hwy24.org/journeys-end.html#:~:text=On%20September%2012%2C%201870%20they,(later%20changed%20to%20Alton); https://ochf.wordpress.com/2012/05/13/hiram-c-bull-1996-inductee-5-2/; https://kansashistoricalsociety.newspapers.com/clip/105937168/bull-city-becomes-alton-on-411885/; https://ochf.wordpress.com/2013/10/07/thomas-marshall-walker-1913-inductee/; Endsley, Niles C. The History of Bull City, 1870-1970. Osborne, KS: Osborne County Farmer, 1970.; McCoy, Sondra Van Meter, and Jan Hults. 1001 Kansas Place Names. University Press of Kansas, 1989.

A Plagiarized Pledge

https://www.newspapers.com/clip/96314797/pledge-of-allegiance-1892/; https://www.smithsonianmag.com/history/the-man-who-wrote-the-pledge-of-allegiance-93907224/; https://www.kshs.org/kansapedia/case-for-the-pledge-of-allegiance/17789; https://www.nytimes.com/2022/04/02/us/pledge-of-allegiance-francis-bellamy.html; https://www.presidency.ucsb.edu/documents/statement-the-president-upon-signing-bill-include-the-words-under-god-the-pledge-the-flag; https://www.legion.org/flag/pledge

Dorothy Gale's Inspiration
https://www.newspapers.com/clip/101743222/
blue-rapids-tornado-account/; https://www.findagrave.
com/memorial/45347831/john-lockwood-gail; https://
moultonmuseum.org/ngm-biography/; https://www.findagrave.
com/memorial/170410067/alta-mchenry; https://www.
findagrave.com/memorial/108529634/flora-aliph-keeney;
http://sites.rootsweb.com/~pasulliv/churches/Annis.htm;
https://stormtrack.org/library/archives/stsep00.htm; https://
archive.org/details/reportoftornadoe00finl; https://www.
mchistory.org/research/biographies/gage-dorothy-louise;
Sandlin, Lee. Storm Kings: The Untold History of America's First
Tornado Chasers. New York: Pantheon Books, 2014.

"Never Take No Cutoffs"
https://www.visitmarysvilleks.org/attraction/alcove-spring/;
https://www.kshs.org/p/the-grave-of-sarah-keyes-on-the-
oregon-trail/12680; https://octa-trails.org/trail-stories/sarah-
keyes-donner-party/; https://www.nps.gov/parkhistory/online_
books/knudsen/sec2a.htm; https://www.oregonencyclopedia.
org/articles/oregon_trail/#.YwWNmOzMLsO; https://www.
laphamsquarterly.org/disaster/miscellany/never-take-no-
cutoffs

Foolhardy Freighters and a Threshing Machine
https://wakeeneytravelblog.wordpress.com/tag/threshing-
machine-canyon/; https://kgi.contentdm.oclc.org/digital/
api/collection/p16884coll113/id/630/download; https://
www.santafetrailresearch.com/research/bod-dispatch.html;
Fitzgerald, Daniel. Ghost Towns of Kansas: A Traveler's Guide.
University Press of Kansas, 1988.

The Gas That Refused to Burn
https://www.acs.org/content/dam/acsorg/education/
whatischemistry/landmarks/heliumnaturalgas/discovery-of-
helium-in-natural-gas-historical-resource.pdf; https://www.
acs.org/content/acs/en/education/whatischemistry/landmarks/
heliumnaturalgas.html#designation-acknowledgments; https://
www.kshs.org/kansapedia/gas-well-in-dexter/12065; https://
todayinsci.com/Events/Chemistry/HeliumKansas.htm; https://
pubmed.ncbi.nlm.nih.gov/22574384/

Finding Black Gold
https://www.sciencedirect.com/topics/earth-and-planetary-
sciences/anticlines; https://www.kgs.ku.edu/Publications/
Bulletins/7/04_hist.html; https://www.kgs.ku.edu/
Publications/Bulletins/7/index.html; https://pubs.er.usgs.gov/
publication/70019374; https://www.wsj.com/articles/the-first-
war-to-run-on-oil-1408045343; https://aoghs.org/petroleum-
pioneers/kansas-oil-boom

Maestro Semiconductor
https://kansassampler.org/8wondersofkansas-people/
jack-kilby-great-bend; https://www.nobelprize.org/
prizes/physics/2000/kilby/biographical/; https://news.
ti.com/blog/2020/09/15/the-chip-that-changed-world;
https://americanhistory.si.edu/collections/search/object/
nmah_689592; https://www.pcworld.com/article/447662/the-
legend-of-jack-kilby-55-years-of-the-integrated-circuit.html

Can You Hear Me Now?
https://www.slate.com/blogs/the_eye/2013/10/03/
strowger_switch_the_19th_century_design_invention_that_
flipped_the_phone.html; https://www.kshs.org/publicat/
history/1982summer_mccoy.pdf; https://dkcohistory.blogspot.
com/2011/01/cl-brown-and-his-affect-on-abilene.html;
https://abilenekansas.org/blog/2020/12/21/cl-brown-kansas-
independent-telephony-and-a-spirit-of-giving; https://www.
sprint.com/companyinfo/history/

Inspiration from a Notebook
https://www.kshs.org/kansapedia/walter-p-chrysler/12015;
https://www.chryslerboyhoodhome.org/; https://www.
thewaltdisneybirthplace.org/2013/12/17/like-father-like-sons-
elias-disney-entrepreneur/; https://chryslerclub.org/walterp.
html; https://ellis.ks.us/travel-tourism/mount-hope-cemetery/

Chrome-Plated Dreams
https://www.salina.com/story/news/2022/02/10/
the-garage-salina-ks-car-museum-opens-downtown-
weekend/6734515001/; https://www.ksn.com/news/
local/salina-classic-car-museum-a-must-see-experience/;
https://salina2020.com/development/american-classics-
auto-museum/; https://www.farmprogress.com/farm-life/
make-tracks-see-garage-salina; https://www.youtube.com/
watch?v=UCdcCBAFQbU

Nostalgia at the Pump
https://roxieontheroad.com/car-culture-in-norton/
https://www.discovernorton.com/tt-about-us

The Planet Hunter
https://www.space.com/19824-clyde-tombaugh.html;
https://www.kshs.org/kansapedia/clyde-tombaugh/12222;
https://kuhistory.ku.edu/articles/planetary-man; https://
lowell.edu/who-was-clyde-tombaugh; https://blogs.k-state.
edu/kansasprofile/2017/07/26/kansas-profile-now-thats-
rural-glen-fountain-pluto-flyby/; https://www.nasa.gov/
feature/15-years-ago-new-horizons-launched-to-pluto-and-
beyond; https://www.nmspacemuseum.org/inductee/clyde-w-
tombaugh/

Fly Me to the Moon
https://www.nasa.gov/sites/default/files/atoms/files/evans_
ronald.pdf; https://spacecenter.org/astronaut-friday-ronald-
evans/; https://kuhistory.ku.edu/articles/fly-us-moon; http://
www.getruralkansas.com/St-Francis/209Explore/1155.shtml;
https://www.nasa.gov/audience/foreducators/spacesuits/
historygallery/ap-dec72a.html; https://blogs.lib.ku.edu/
spencer/throwback-thursday-ku-astronaut-edition/

The Dream That Failed to Fly
http://www.aerofiles.com/mayfly-sidebar.
html; https://www.physicsclassroom.com/class/
newtlaws/Lesson-4/Newton-s-Third-Law; https://
roxieontheroad.com/copter/; https://pdfpiw.uspto.gov/.
piw?Docid=01028781&homeurl=http%3A%2F%2Fpatft.
uspto.gov%2Fnetacgi%2Fnph-Parser%3FSect1%3DPTO1%2
526Sect2%3DHITOFF%2526d%3DPALL%2526p%3D1%252
6u%3D%25252Fnetahtml%25252FPTO%25252Fsrchnum.
htm%2526r%3D1%2526f%3DG%2526l%3D50%
2526s1%3D1028781.
PN.%25260S%3DPN%2F1028781%2526RS%
3DPN%2F1028781&PageNum=&Rtype=
&SectionNum=&idkey=
NONE&Input=View+first+page; Farris, Mary Collett. The Short

Happy Life of the Kansas Flying Machine. Goodland, KS: High Plains Museum, 1982.

Amelia and *Muriel*
https://www.atchisonglobenow.com/news/local_news/muriels-journey/article_bb46171f-2451-5baf-857b-fabab697b08a.html; https://ameliaearharthangarmuseum.org/muriel/; https://www.atchisonglobenow.com/news/local_news/thousands-line-the-streets-to-see-amelia-years-ago/article_bbe46acf-8fbf-5c87-8abb-55b7e2b20be7.html; https://www.nytimes.com/2017/07/18/us/amelia-earhart-kansas-hometown-mystery-birthday.html; https://ameliaearharthangarmuseum.org/bringing-ae-to-dc/; https://www.ameliaearhartmuseum.org/

Touch Down at the Beaumont Hotel
https://beaumonthotelks.com/; https://roxieontheroad.com/stay-at-the-beaumont-hotel-a-historic-oasis/

The Man Who Saved the Mail
https://www.findagrave.com/memorial/39447751/clarence-audburn-gilbert; https://postalmuseum.si.edu/gilbert-clarence-a; https://www.newspapers.com/clip/21444880/plainville-times/; https://www.airmailpioneers.org/content/Pilots/Gilbert.htm; https://dolearchivecollections.ku.edu/collections/speeches/004/c019_004_002_all.pdf; https://rookscounty.net/rooks-co-museum/

"No Mail, Low Morale"
https://www.aarp.org/home-family/voices/veterans/info-2020/wwii-hero-central-postal-directory.html; https://history.army.mil/html/topics/afam/6888thPBn/index.html; https://www.nps.gov/mamc/the-6888th-central-postal-directory-battalion.htm; https://www.armyupress.army.mil/Journals/Military-Review/English-Edition-Archives/Jan-Feb-2019/Warrington-Mail/

Super Spreader
https://www.ncbi.nlm.nih.gov/pmc/articles/PMC1999792/pdf/pubhealthreporig03239-0001.pdf; https://ghjournalsearch.org/resources/public-health-reports; https://www.cdc.gov/flu/pandemic-resources/1918-commemoration/1918-pandemic-history.htm; https://history.army.mil/covid19/Spanish-Flu1918_On-Point-Magazine-Dr-Bob-Smith.pdf; https://www.nationalguard.mil/News/News-Features/Article/1616713/flu-outbreak-killed-45000-us-soldiers-during-world-war-i/; https://storymaps.arcgis.com/stories/7469c254b14f4241b14d485f49742260; https://www.kshs.org/publicat/history/2020summer_grant.pdf; https://www.kshs.org/kansapedia/camp-funston/16692

The Ultimate Quack
https://www.casemine.com/judgement/us/5914a634add7b049346d73d9; https://www.kcur.org/politics-elections-and-government/2018-08-09/the-last-time-a-kansas-gubernatorial-election-was-this-close-it-involved-goat-glands; http://plainshumanities.unl.edu/encyclopedia/doc/egp.med.006; http://www.gchsweb.org/

Take Your Medicine
https://www.crispinsdrugstoremuseum.com/; https://thequackdoctor.com/index.php/bomb-the-first-sneeze-with-kilacold/; https://www.healthline.com/health/bloodletting; https://americanhistory.si.edu/collections/search/object/

nmah_719929; https://www.ncbi.nlm.nih.gov/pmc/articles/PMC2844275/

"The Little Nurse for Little Ills"
https://www.kshs.org/publicat/history/2011spring_miner.pdf; https://www.kshs.org/kansapedia/albert-alexander-hyde/16907; https://www.visitleavenworthks.com/visitors/page/sister-city-program; https://www.reporterherald.com/2017/08/02/mentholatum-inventor-made-cold-cash-and-used-his-profits-for-good/; https://visit-omi.com/people/article/william-merrell-vories

"The Healthiest State in the Union"
https://klcjournal.com/the-colorful-contentious-story-behind-health-advocate-samuel-crumbines-leadership/; https://www.kshs.org/kansapedia/samuel-j-crumbine/12025 https://kuhistory.ku.edu/articles/%E2%80%9Cwho-would-command-greater-respect%E2%80%9D; https://www.kshs.org/kansapedia/milburn-stone/18145; https://theinventors.org/library/inventors/blflyswatter.htm; https://krwa.net/portals/krwa/lifeline/2011/DontSpitOnTheSidewalk.pdf

Stand and Deliver in Teacher Town USA
https://www.kcur.org/2017-08-04/theres-a-national-teachers-hall-of-fame-who-knew; https://www.nthf.org/; https://www.cjonline.com/story/entertainment/local/2009/03/08/did-you-know/16469051007/; https://nthfmemorial.org/; https://www.nthf.org/1999-cohort.html; https://visitemporia.com/place/one-room-school-house/; https://www.nthf.org/falleneducators.html

Birthplace of Kansas Day
https://www.kansasmemory.org/item/220347/; https://www.kshs.org/kansapedia/kansas-day/16773; https://www.kshs.org/kansapedia/kansas-day-an-alternate-anniversary/19918; https://kansashistoricalsociety.newspapers.com/clip/108500279/kansas-day-in-bird-city/; https://kansashistoricalsociety.newspapers.com/clip/108501444/kansas-day-should-be-a-state-holiday/; http://www.nwkansas.com/BCwebpages/Pdf%20pages%20-%20all/bc%20pages-pdfs%202010/bcPages_01_Jan/Week4/BC%20Front-04.pdf

The Bison's Savior
https://www.nationalbuffalofoundation.org/hall-of-fame-honorees/charles-jesse-buffalo-jones; https://www.jstor.org/stable/23531808?read-now=1&refreqid=excelsior%3Aec205c452f83e984e7824c0a1e7f595b#page_scan_tab_contents; https://cdapress.com/news/2017/jul/20/buffalo-jones-hunter-cowboy-and-icon-of-the-5/; https://www.visitgck.com/buffalo-jones-a-finney-county-hero/; https://www.mtpr.org/arts-culture/2017-01-30/the-hornaday-bison-killing-buffalo-in-order-to-save-them; https://www.ozarkbisons.com/aboutbison.php; Thomas, Phillip Drennon. Buffalo Jones: Citizen of the Kansas Frontier. Garden City, KS: Finney County Historical Museum, 2004.

The Forest That Didn't Take
https://www.kshs.org/kansapedia/kansas-national-forest/12119; https://archive.org/details/conquestofsouthw00blan; https://ksoutdoors.com/KDWP-Info/Locations/Wildlife-Areas/Southwest/Sandsage-Bison-Range/History; https://roadsandkingdoms.com/2016/a-

forest-built-by-hand/; https://digitalcommons.unl.edu/greatplainsquarterly/2430/

When the Bride Came Home to Cottonwood Ranch
https://www.kshs.org/p/cottonwood-ranch/19571; https://www.cottonwoodranchks.com/; https://www.kshs.org/kansapedia/john-fenton-pratt/15162; https://www.kshs.org/kansapedia/pratt-family/12177; https://www.cottonwoodranchks.com/family-stories.html; https://www.kshs.org/resource/national_register/nominationsNRDB/Sheridan_PrattJohnFentonRanchNR.pdf

Putting Wheat in the Wheat State
https://www.ksgenweb.org/archives/1912/w3/warkentin_bernard.html; https://www.kshs.org/kansapedia/bernard-warkentin/15595; https://www.jstor.org/stable/3627314; https://ia800300.us.archive.org/28/items/impactofmennonit00mart/impactofmennonit00mart.pdf

Creepy Crawlies
https://www.travelawaits.com/2558428/best-things-to-do-in-manhattan-kansas/; https://www.k-state.edu/butterfly/; https://www.manhattancvb.com/listing/insect-zoo/70/; https://www.k-state.edu/gardens/; https://www.youtube.com/watch?v=7bUvp2On6yU; https://www.youtube.com/watch?v=hoB3Qjwg9mg

The Octagonal Vegetarians
https://kansashistoricalsociety.newspapers.com/clip/37019832/octagon-city-story-of-the-founders; https://kansashistoricalsociety.newspapers.com/clip/37019457/octagon-city-initial-plans/; https://kansaspublicradio.org/blog/kpr-staff/name-kansas-ghost-town-july-25-2014; https://news.google.com/newspapers?id=hfofAAAAIBAJ&pg=977%2C3053561; Colt, Miriam Davis. Went to Kansas. Watertown, NY: L. Ingalls, 1862.; Fitzgerald, Daniel. Ghost Towns of Kansas: A Traveler's Guide. University Press of Kansas, 1988.

Don't Compete with the James Gang
http://www.oldmeadecounty.com/hideout1.htm; https://www.kshs.org/resource/national_register/nominationsNRDB/Meade_DaltonGangHideoutandMuseumNR.pdf; https://www.ksn.com/news/local/main-street-kansas/dalton-gang-hideout-digs-into-historic-tunnel/; https://www.coffeyville.com/514/The-Dalton-Raid-Story; https://kansashistoricalsociety.newspapers.com/clip/109053812/robber-gang-meets-their-waterloo/; https://www.nps.gov/articles/coffeyville-kansas-the-town-that-stopped-the-dalton-gang-teaching-with-historic-places.htm; https://www.coffeyvillehistory.com/the-dalton-museum

The Fatal Fingerprint
https://www.gcpolice.org/about-gcpd/history/famous-cases/jake-fleagle; https://thegreathighprairie.com/the-fleagle-gang-and-the-fingerprint-that-proved-their-guilt/; https://thelibrary.org/lochist/periodicals/wrv/V7/N1/F79e.htm; https://www.canyonsandplains.com/the-fleagle-gang-violence-on-the-plains; https://www.irmamagazines.com/wp-content/uploads/2018/10/CL-2018-ctgy-2-Historic-34999-or-less.pdf; https://www.kansascommerce.gov/2019/04/bonnie-clyde-in-hugoton-ks-new-medicine-findings-inspire-kumc-exhibit-open-to-the-public-through-may/; Betz,

N[orman].T. The Fleagle Gang: Betrayed by a Fingerprint. Bloomington, IN: AuthorHouse, 2005.

The Vanishing Serial Killers
https://slate.com/news-and-politics/2022/03/bloody-benders-true-story-kate-bender-crimes-susan-jonusas.html; https://nypost.com/2022/03/26/how-a-serial-killer-family-murdered-8-and-got-away-with-it/; https://www.kshs.org/kansapedia/kate-bender/11980; https://truewestmagazine.com/history-mystery-solved-hiding-in-plain-sight/

Artist Provocateur
https://www.nytimes.com/2017/08/23/arts/mt-liggett-86-folk-artist-and-provocateur-is-dead.html; https://klcjournal.com/liggett-last-laugh/; https://www.uplandexhibits.com/work/mt-liggett/; https://rawvision.com/blogs/articles/articles-prairie-provocateur; https://hayspost.com/posts/5eb5967feb7f17053604882e; https://www.mtliggettartenvironment.org/home; http://www.kohlerfoundation.org/preservation/preserved-sites/m-t-liggett/; https://www.bigwell.org/

Fine Art from Found Objects
https://www.kshs.org/kansapedia/lester-wilton-raymer/19977; https://www.redbarnstudio.org/; https://tfaoi.org/aa/10aa/10aa445.htm; https://www.askart.com/auction_records/Lester_Wilton_Raymer/116215/Lester_Wilton_Raymer.aspx

Walk with the Dinosaurs
https://www.eriekansastourism.com/; http://spacesarchives.org/explore/search-the-online-collection/robert-dorris-dinosaur-not-so-national-park/; https://www.fourstateshomepage.com/news/final-exhibit-installed-at-erie-dinosaur-park/; https://eriedinosaurpark.wixsite.com/roadsideattractions; https://www.forbeshoffman.com/obituary/163471; https://www.chanute.com/obituaries/article_183920be-3b09-11e9-b456-5b73c9694189.html

Art of the Fossils
https://www.visitoakleyks.com/fick-fossil-history-museum; https://fickfossilmuseum.wordpress.com/2013/09/25/autumn-artwork-by-vi-fick/; https://www.youtube.com/watch?v=P7wDtY0txx8; https://www.kake.com/story/47053820/western-kansas-was-hells-aquarium-80-million-years-ago-heres-what-it-can-teach-us-today

Monster Mash
https://www.facebook.com/Eyegorescuriosities; https://www.atlasobscura.com/places/eyegores-odditorium-and-monster-museum; https://www.ksn.com/gooddaykansas/eyegores-odditorium-and-monster-museum/; https://www.facebook.com/eyegoresodditorium; Matt Alford (Owner) in discussion with the author, April 2022

Alone in a Cage
https://wichitalifeict.com/wichita-troll/; https://www.360wichita.com/blog/Local/Wichita-Troll.html; https://botanica.org/sleepy-troll-hill/; https://sculpturenews.tumblr.com/post/84063819674/wichita-troll-by-connie-ernatt-reinstalled-after/amp

Dream Horizon
https://www.wichita.edu/academics/fine_arts/adci/news/2019/dale_small_horizontes.php; https://www.

horizontes-project.com/; https://orioleonline.com/3429/news/
wichita-welcomes-record-breaking-mural/; https://www.kmuw.
org/community/2019-01-25/to-paint-a-mural-horizontes-
project-helps-north-wichitans-see-in-color

How to Paint the Town
https://youtu.be/f_ecAk1i9xc -; https://www.wibw.
com/2022/06/15/clay-center-welcome-25th-mural-over-
summer-with-special-connection/; https://www.ksre.k-state.
edu/news/stories/2021/06/kansas-profile-a-mural-movement.
html; https://www.uncoveringkansas.com/episodes; https://
www.farmprogress.com/farm-life/clay-centers-mural-
movement-stands-out-skyline; https://www.cstanleycreative.
com/copy-of-lemonade-rhino

Out of the Box
https://www.visitgck.com/things-to-do/boy-scouts-of-america-
jessie-montes-art-gallery/; https://www.joplinglobe.com/news/
lifestyles/cardboard-clipper-jesse-montes-out-of-the-box-
features-unique-3-d-works/article_4551b444-7931-5fe2-
96dc-3a7e984bfc9c.html; http://stauthmemorialmuseum.
org/event/cardboard-creations-jessie-montez/; https://
sanangelfolkart.com/montes/index.htm; https://www.
grassrootsart.net/25year-pg5; https://www.chieftain.com/
story/opinion/columns/2005/04/24/lord-board/8468677007/

Married to Adventure
https://safarimuseum.com/; https://kansaslivingmagazine.com/
attraction/martin-and-osa-johnson-safari-museum; https://
www.kshs.org/kansapedia/martin-and-osa-johnson/12102;
https://wfpp.columbia.edu/pioneer/ccp-osa-johnson/; https://
kansasleadershipcenter.org/martin-and-osa-johnson/; https://
www.jstor.org/stable/44252197?mag=how-two-kansans-
invented-the-safari-documentary&seq=4#metadata_info_tab_
contents; https://artsandsciences.utulsa.edu/osa-johnson-
wgs-lindstrom/; Johnson, Osa. I Married Adventure: The Lives
of Martin and Osa Johnson. New York: Kodansha America, Inc.,
1997.

Climbing the Learning Tree
https://www.kshs.org/kansapedia/gordon-parks/12164;
https://www.tkaahistorytrail.org/gordon-parks-museum/;
https://www.artic.edu/artists/20027/gordon-parks; https://
iphf.org/inductees/gordon-parks/; https://www.pbs.org/
newshour/show/photogs-hunt-childhood-friends-reveals-
1940s-black-life-segregation

Surrounded by Art
https://www.nermanmuseum.org/_resources/pdfs/nerman-
orientation-guide.pdf; https://www.nermanmuseum.org/;
https://www.youtube.com/watch?v=5SZJWfMkjPQ; https://
www.jccc.edu/about/campus/maps/buildings/nmoca.html

Where Fashion Sits
https://www.jccc.edu/academics/credit/fashion-
merchandising-design/fashion-design-collection.html;
https://www.kcur.org/arts-life/2021-11-19/hats-and-shoes-
and-dresses-pave-a-trip-down-memory-lane-at-johnson-
county-museums-all-electric-house; https://www.jccc.edu/
events/2022/0909-nerman-adorned.html

The Last Piece of Kanzas
https://kawnation.com/?page_id=7508; https://www.kshs.org/
kansapedia/allegawaho/19397; https://kansashistoricalsociety.

newspapers.com/clip/108627095/frank-haucke-adopted/;
https://www.robinsonpark1929.com/; https://kawnation.
com/wp-content/uploads/2018/11/KanzaWhoUnit-Student-
Activities.pdf; https://www.kshs.org/resource/national_
register/MPS/KS_KanzaPeopleofKansas_statewideMPDF_
listed08012021.pdf

The Great Settlement and the Last Conquistador
https://etzanoa.com/etzanoa/; https://www.sciencenews.org/
article/drones-native-american-settlement-etzanoa-kansas-
pasture; https://www.latimes.com/nation/la-na-kansas-lost-
city-20180819-htmlstory.html; https://open.upress.virginia.
edu/read/before-american-history/section/f7ed341e-ff76-
4eb8-8266-8f6df86fbe39; https://the-shocker.wichita.
edu/story.php?eid=60&id=1632#.YxkSTezMLs0; https://
indiancountrytoday.com/archive/lost-city-etzanoa-found

A Refuge Far from Home
https://www.kshs.org/p/migration-of-the-pueblo-people-
to-el-cuartelejo/16733; https://www.kshs.org/teachers/
project_archaeology/pdfs/migration_teacher_guide.pdf;
https://www.kshs.org/p/migration-of-the-pueblo-people-to-el-
cuartelejo/16733; https://www.kshs.org/resource/national_
register/nominationsNRDB/Scott_ElCuartelejoNR.pdf; http://
www.picurispueblo.org/home.html; Treib, Marc. Sanctuaries
of Spanish New Mexico. Berkeley, CA: University of California
Press, 1993.; Calloway, Colin Gordon. One Vast Winter Count:
The Native American West Before Lewis and Clark. Lincoln, NE:
University of Nebraska Press, 2003.

From Sacred to Submerged
https://www.newspapers.com/clip/21889064/legend-
of-waconda-to-die-under-glen/; https://www.glenelder.
com/waconda-springs.html; https://sunflowerstateradio.
com/2019/03/25/waconda-springs-replica-to-be-renovated/;
https://www.glenelder.com/history-of-ge-dam.html;
https://krex.k-state.edu/dspace/bitstream/handle/2097/
41106/2a3fb102edd10f5f6f1cff69591e2663.
pdf?sequence=1&isAllowed=y; https://themercury.com/
news/a-look-back-at-the-1951-flood-70-years-later/
article_29d52f24-ecca-5fb3-9d9f-d6635792e578.html

The Last Kansas Reservoir
https://blogs.k-state.edu/kansasprofile/2022/03/02/audrey-
rupp-horsethief-reservoir/; https://horsethiefreservoir.com/
about-us/; https://agriculture.ks.gov/docs/default-source/
dwr-ws-fact-sheets/history-of-dams.pdf?sfvrsn=ffd7aac1_6;
https://mjellc.net/casestudies/horsethief-reservoir/; https://
www.swaimfuneralhome.com/obituary/658641

To the Glory of God
https://www.damarcommunityhistoricalfoundation.org/history-
ancestry/; https://kansassampler.org/8wondersofkansas-arch/;
https://salinadiocese.org/parish/st-joseph-parish-damar/;
https://rookscounty.net/historic-church-and-art-tour/; https://
conradschmitt.com/project/st-joseph-catholic-damar-kansas/;
https://www.kshs.org/kansapedia/henry-w-brinkman/18222;
Brian Newell (Mayor) in discussion with the author, October
2007; Kaylon Roberts (President, Damar Community Historical
Foundation) in discussion with the author, November 2021

Promise Kept
https://saintaloysius.weebly.com/; https://jesuitarchives.
omeka.net/items/show/238; https://www.acatholicmission.
org/father-philip-colleton.html; https://www.findagrave.com/
memorial/227014658/philip_phillipe-colleton

Treats without Tricks
https://www.hiawathaworldonline.com/special_sections/100-
years-of-tradition-how-it-all-began-with-mrs-krebs/
article_ca12522b-5176-5ad8-86f9-a8cd4613f37f.
html; https://www.cityofhiawatha.org/visitors/halloween-
frolic; https://kansashistoricalsociety.newspapers.com/
clip/108266024/halloween-frolic-is-a-success/; https://www.
hiawathaworldonline.com/special_sections/
the-halloween-queens/article_bf0c0e29-917c-
5766-abb2-4a17d0b2ec52.html; https://www.findagrave.com/
memorial/66015125/elizabeth-krebs

Elkhart's Olympic Glory
http://www.civics.ks.gov/kansas/kansans/olympic-athletes.
html; https://ks.milesplit.com/articles/234202/kansan-
trackxc-archetypes-dr-glenn-cunningham-phd; https://union.
ku.edu/glenn-cunningham; https://www.kstatesports.com/
news/2021/5/11/sports-extra-se-69-years-later-thane-baker-
reflects-on-olympic-debut-as-k-state-junior.aspx; https://
mtcoks.com/247/Museum

A Teter That Won't Totter
https://newprairiepress.org/cgi/viewcontent.
cgi?referer=&httpsredir=1&article=1101&context=sfh;
https://www.iolaregister.com/news/striving-for-the-pinnacle;
https://www.travelks.com/blog/stories/post/time-at-teter-
rock/; https://www.mrhinsurance.com/teter-rock.html

Diamonds Are a Hotel's Best Friend
https://www.grandcentralhotel.com/; https://www.aaa.com/
travelinfo/kansas/cottonwood-falls/hotels/grand-central-
hotel-94417.html; https://www.emporiagazette.com/news/
article_55c37802-c46b-58f7-bb0f-c1ca1e4e8751.html;
https://www.nytimes.com/1998/07/26/travel/a-prairie-home.
html

Suzan Barnes (Owner) in discussion with the author, May 2017,
May 2019, and March 2022

The Ultimate Man Cave
https://www.travelawaits.com/2679028/ellinwood-
kansas-underground-city/; https://www.ksal.com/
ellinwood-underground-tour/; https://kansassampler.
org/8wondersofkansas-customs/connecting-underground-
businesses-ellinwood; https://www.ellinwoodchamber.com/
ellinwood-underground-tunnels

American Bandstand
https://www.cityofiola.com/232/Municipal-Band-Concerts;
https://www.iolaregister.com/news/new-direction-for-
a-music-tradition; https://www.iolachamber.org/events/
ice-cream-socials.html; https://americanprofile.com/articles/
kansas-oldest-town-band-playing-since-1871/

INDEX

178